The
Fallacy
Detective

The Fallacy Detective

Thirty-Six Lessons on How to Recognize Bad Reasoning

by Nathaniel Bluedorn
& Hans Bluedorn

March 2003
CHRISTIAN LOGIC

The Fallacy Detective
by Nathaniel Bluedorn and Hans Bluedorn

Library of Congress Control Number: 2003090416

Christian Logic
PMB 168, 429 Lake Park Blvd.
Muscatine, Iowa 52761
309-537-3641
www.christianlogic.com

Trivium Pursuit
PMB 168, 429 Lake Park Blvd.
Muscatine, Iowa 52761
309-537-3641
www.triviumpursuit.com

"Thou shalt not muzzle the ox that treadeth out the corn. And, The labourer is worthy of his reward." – 1 Timothy 5:18 (1 Corinthians 9:9; Deuteronomy 25:4; Luke 10:7; Matthew 10:10; Deuteronomy 24:15)

"Therefore, behold, I am against the prophets, saith the LORD, that steal my words every one from his neighbour." – Jeremiah 23:30

"...Thou shalt not steal,...Thou shalt love thy neighbour as thyself." – Romans 13:9 (Matthew 19:18; Mark 10:19; Luke 18:20; 1 Corinthians 6:8,10; Ephesians 4:28; Exodus 20:15; Leviticus 19:11,13; Deuteronomy 5:19; Leviticus 19:18; Matthew 5:43, 7:12, 19:19, 22:39; Mark 12:31; Luke 10:27; Galatians 5:14; James 2:8)

"Render therefore to all their dues:...honour to whom honour." – Romans 13:7

"That no man go beyond and defraud his brother in any matter: because that the Lord is the avenger of all such, as we also have forewarned you and testified." – 1 Thessalonians 4:6 (Leviticus 19:13; Deuteronomy 32:35; Proverbs 22:22,23)

Any resemblances in this book
to any person, place, or thing
– living or dead –
just might be on purpose.

Many thanks to our sister Johannah,
who drew "Toodles" the detective for us.

Contents

4 Making Assumptions

5 Statistical Fallacies

6 Propaganda

7 The Fallacy Detective Game

8 Answer Key

1

Introduction

What Is a Fallacy?

A fallacy is an error in logic – a place where someone has made a mistake in his thinking.

EXAMPLE

> Dad: "People just don't use their heads anymore."
> Johnny: "I don't know about that, Dad. I use my head a lot playing soccer."

Dad and Johnny are talking about two different ways of using heads.

This book is for detectives – fallacy detectives. We've designed this book to be a handy manual for learning to spot common errors in reasoning. The goal of this book is to help answer the question: *What is bad reasoning?* We also hope you will find that logic can be fun.

To begin this book, we first show why it is important to stretch and exercise your mind. Then we divide the most common errors in reasoning into three sections with twenty-three lessons. We explain how you can spot these errors, and we give exercises to stretch your abilities at fallacy detection. This is followed by a section on propaganda techniques which are commonly used in the media and advertisements, as well as by politicians. The book ends with *The Fallacy Detective Game*, where you can have fun with your friends who have been learning logic with you.

When you complete this book, you should be able to:

1. Put a high value on good reasoning.
2. Know how to spot many forms of bad reasoning.
3. Know how to avoid using many fallacies in your own reasoning.

The Vision of Christian Logic

Who are we? We are brothers – Nathaniel Bluedorn and Hans Bluedorn. We have been homeschooled all our lives. Since 1989, our family has given workshops on homeschooling and classical education in forty-four states. Out of this has developed our family business, Trivium Pursuit, through which we produce educational materials for homeschoolers. Christian logic and apologetics have always been important to our family, and beginning in 1999, we boys began to focus our attention on making these subjects more available to Christians.

Why are we doing this? We see a need for Christians to strive for a higher standard of reasoning. We believe God wants his people to become aware of their lack of discernment, and logic is an important part of the science of discernment. For instance, many Christians adopt beliefs and practices without properly evaluating the arguments which are used to support them. We need to rediscover the way of the Bereans, who searched the Scriptures daily to see if the apostles' teaching were true (Acts 17:10-11).

As we grow older, we become more aware of how poor many people's reasoning is. But we also need to realize how poor *our own* reasoning is. This is a humbling thought, and with it we embark on a journey towards higher standards of reasoning. We will never be as logical as the Lord Jesus Christ was, but we must work at it.

But besides just learning logic, we also see a need for a truly Christian logic. Our challenge is to define good reasoning in a truly biblical way. Logic was not invented by a pagan philosopher named Aristotle. Logic is the science of thinking the way God thinks – the way Jesus taught us to think.

We also need to have inquiring minds. Our parents taught us a love for knowledge, and they challenged us to use our minds. We want to communicate this love to others.

How This Book Is Different

This book is for Christians. We have tried to interweave a genuinely Christian worldview into this book. The subject of logic will greatly influence a person's private philosophy and view of life. Therefore, we believe it is important that Christians learn their reasoning skills from a genuinely Christian worldview.

This book focuses on practical logic. This book teaches you to recognize the logical fallacies which you meet every day in the street, or in the newspaper, or in your work. Thousands of years ago, the Greek philosopher Aristotle began to study and categorize these common errors in reasoning. Ever since that time, people have found this branch of logic to be the most interesting and useful in ordinary life.

Branches of Logic

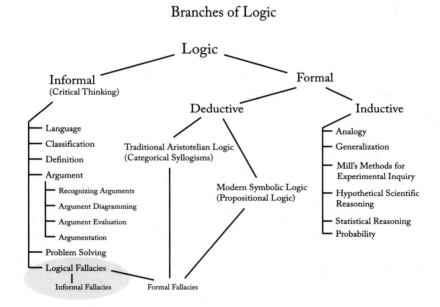

We are indebted to James B. Nance for part of this diagram.

As you can see by the circle in this diagram, we do not cover all branches of logic in this book. All of the other branches, including syllogisms, scientific reasoning, argumentation, etc., are very useful. But we chose informal logical fallacies as the focus of this book.

This book is self-teaching. We have tried to make this book doable for everyday people. You should be able to work through this book without needing outside help. We want logic to be available and understandable to everybody.

How to Use This Book

Who Should Use This Book?

This book is for children and parents to use together. Thinking is something which everybody does, and if children learn logic, but their parents do not – well, that is a subject for discussion. If you as a parent tell your child that he is now going to study some logic, but you tell him that you do not have the time to learn it with him, then what message are you giving him? If logic is something good to learn, then why doesn't everybody in the family learn it?

The picture we had in mind when we wrote this book was of a father or mother sitting beside the children and working through this book together. Parents and children all read the chapter, they all discuss it, and they all do the exercises together.

What About Classroom Schools?

Since we first wrote this book, we have received many letters from teachers who have used our book in their school classroom. While we did not have this in mind when we wrote our book, we have learned that the picture of parents and children works equally well with a teacher in a classroom. For some tips on how to use this book in a classroom, visit our website www.christianlogic.com.

What Ages Is This Book For?

In our experience, most children learn logic best when they are thirteen years or older. Therefore, we have designed this book for students age thirteen and above. There is no maximum age, so grandparents have no excuse.

How Difficult Will This Book Be?

We know that logic is a new subject to most people, so we wrote this book to be your teacher. We designed the lesson format to contain many concrete examples, and we included exercises for many levels of difficulty. In this way, the concepts are easy to understand, and the skills are easy to learn.

Actually, we like to think of it this way – our book helps you to discover the logic which is already written in your mind by God. We only make you more aware of the logic which you've been using all of your life.

What Is the Lesson Format?

Each lesson begins with a section for you to read, and ends with exercises for you to answer. As we hinted at before, there are different ways you can use our book to fit your situation. Here are a few suggestions.

We recommend that you work through this book in a group of two or more people. There is something about multiple people discussing their agreements or disagreements which brings out so much more in the lesson. You may wish to have each person read each lesson independently, then have everyone go through the lesson together.

As you read each exercise and give your answer, you can check each answer with the answer key provided at the back of this book. As you follow this three-step sequence (first read the exercise, then give your answer, then check your answer), you will have your answers immediately corrected if you happen to miss the point.

If you have trouble understanding a lesson, then do the exercises for that lesson anyway. We designed the exercises to be a teaching tool, so you may catch in the exercises what you did not understand in the lesson itself. If you miss many of the exercises, and you do not know why, then you may need to repeat a lesson until you understand it. If you still don't understand something taught in this book, then try discussing it with other people. You may find other students at our web site www.christianlogic.com. You can share your misery, and maybe find an answer.

Here Is the Challenge

Remember, most people never study good thinking skills. So people who take on this quest of learning logic are breaking out of the mold, and this takes courage. It also takes humility. But most of all, it takes self-discipline.

2

The Inquiring Mind

Lesson 1

Exercise Your Mind

If we've written this book to answer the question *what is bad reasoning*, then we should begin by asking *what is good reasoning*? This first section will bring out three qualities or standards of good reasoning. Our Dad and Mom always wanted us children to have "inquiring minds." We'll try to introduce you to some of the things which they taught us.

The first problem which we need to address is this: Most people don't like to use their minds – period. Everyone loves to have fun, and some of us even love to work. But we all try to avoid using our minds as much as possible. Hopefully, we can change that.

EXAMPLE A

Mother to her son: "Dear, Dad and I have been talking, and we feel that it isn't good for you to spend so much time playing video games. We feel that, as your parents, we should help you develop your mind…"

Johnny: "Wooah! Cool! One blast! Get this! I'm in the 72nd level, and the Zygon-clone Monster is going to eat my neutrino-grenades in a moment. Look…"

Mother: "Could you pause that game for a moment and listen to me? I'm trying to talk to you about your future."

Johnny: "What if I want to be a fighter pilot when I grow up, and these games will help hand-eye coordination?"

Mother: "It's hard to talk to you rationally while…"

Johnny: "Hang on there, I'm coming to where I have to jump and shoot at the same…"

Mother: "I've been doing some reading about what video games do to the brain. They've done studies that show that…"

Johnny: "Jeepers! He almost got me! If I can make it around…"

Johnny's mother is trying to get Johnny to engage his mind, but that is exactly what Johnny doesn't want to do. He is having fun, and his game is using as much of his mind as he wants to use.

"So teach us to number our days,
    that we may apply our hearts unto wisdom."
    Psalm 90:12 (KJV)

When a person gets old enough to realize how short his life is, then he begins to realize how valuable it would have been if he had learned wisdom early in life. When Johnny gets as old as his Mom and Dad are now, then he will understand why his parents tried so hard to teach him to exercise his mind. Johnny's Mom and Dad probably don't want to make the same mistake with their son as their parents made with them.

"The heart of him that hath understanding seeketh knowledge:
    but the mouth of fools feedeth on foolishness."
    Proverbs 15:14 (KJV)

"Wisdom is the principal thing; therefore get wisdom:
    and with all thy getting get understanding."
    Proverbs 4:7 (KJV)

One of the most important lessons in the book of Proverbs is that we should work hard to use our minds to understand things. This means we'll need to make our minds do some stretches! And if there is only one thing you learn from this book, we want to inspire you to exercise your mind – and not let it get fat and flabby.

EXAMPLE B

Farmer Ed: "Like I told your father, your aunt Mabel and I haven't made a profit from the farm for years now."

Young Nephew back from Agricultural College: "Why don't you try changing some of the way you do things on your farm?"

Farmer Ed: "I think I'll just stick to what I've got going right now. I don't have the patience to try this new system you're talking about – I'd have to unlearn a lot. Your grandpa always said you can't teach an old dog new tricks. I like your optimism – farming needs people like you – but we're pretty settled here at the farm."

Farmer Ed looks at his nephew's new ideas and he sees too much hard mental work. He doesn't believe he has the energy to rethink all that he's learned about farming. Farmer Ed might be willing to do the physical work, but it takes mental work to change, and that's what he's afraid of. Thinking is hard work.

The mind is like a muscle. It needs exercise, too.

As Christians, we have the opportunity – the obligation – to use our minds to serve God. We must discipline our minds the same way an athlete exercises his body. We must exercise our minds so that it does not hurt anymore when we try to use them. This is the first quality of an *inquiring mind*.

Exercises

Read the following examples, and decide if the person probably: (a) doesn't want to exercise his mind or is afraid of the mental work which it takes to make changes, (b) has an inquiring mind, or (c) none of the above.

1. Surfer Dude: "Hey, man. Like, these waves are, like, so cool, I just can, like, spend my life here, man. Like, this is, like, life, man."

2. A Little Child: "I can't pick up my toys… I don't remember where they go."

3. Ted: "Don't make me go into town to pick up groceries. There's a foot of snow fall since last night, and it will be a pain to shovel out the driveway again."

4. Bradley: "My grandpa tried to get me to go to one of those political debates again."
    Wesson: "Yeah? You mean between the guys running for mayor? What'd you tell him?"
    Bradley: "He knows I don't go in for that stuff. I don't get what they say. Like, uh, who wants to?"

5. Merle: "I like reading two different newspapers which report the same event. That way I see the issue from two perspectives."

6. Blaine: "Oh, Dad, do I have to? I hate mowing the lawn. I get covered with grass and my allergies start to bother me."

7. Newt: "I hate going to the library. I always get caught into reading some book and wasting a lot of time. But let's go anyway."

8. Benny: "If I don't finish reading this book tonight, I'll have to pay the library fine."

Lesson 2

Love to Listen

This lesson is about listening and the benefits that come from listening. Some people just don't like to listen. You don't want to be like that.

EXAMPLE A

One day, Bob goes over to a friend's house for a potluck dinner. Afterwards, Bob notices a circle of the guys over in the corner having a discussion. He catches a snatch of what they're talking about, and he interjects a few thoughts on the advantages of old farm tractors.

After several minutes, Bob pauses. There is silence among the former conversants – as they try to imagine where he is coming from. They had been discussing the difference between male and female car drivers – not farm machinery. Bob chalks their silence up to shyness, and he starts talking again on little-known facts about farm machinery.

As the men begin to drift away, Bob becomes more and more animated – he thinks they must not be getting what he is saying. The remaining men wait for a pause to interrupt Bob courteously. Finally, one man shrugs, mumbles something about getting somewhere on time, and strolls away. Everybody else does the same.

What is Bob's problem? Is it that Bob just talks too much? People who know Bob might agree. However, is it possible that his problem is deeper? Can it be that Bob simply does not like to listen – he enjoys telling people what he thinks more than he enjoys listening to what they have to say?

"A wise man will hear, and will increase in learning,
And a man of understanding will acquire wise counsel…"
Proverbs 1:5 (NASB)

In this verse Solomon tells us that wise men try to listen to others and that is how they learn things. A spirit of listening goes a long way to communicate an attitude of humility.

"...everyone must be quick to hear, slow to speak..."
James 1:19 (NASB)

"The way of a fool is right in his own eyes,
But a wise man is he who listens..."
Proverbs 12:15 (NASB)

A person who is humble, and who loves to listen, may show these characteristics:

1. He is more interested in hearing what other people have to say than in having them listen to him. Humility brings respect for others and for their thoughts.
2. He places a modest value on his own opinions – he admits that other people often have better ideas than he does.
3. He willingly admits when he doesn't know something. If he doesn't understand something, he is open about it.
4. He is willing to question his own position on an issue.

If a person shows these qualities, then he may be someone who loves to listen. And being a person who loves to listen is another ingredient to having an *inquiring mind*.

Exercises

Are the people in the following examples (a) showing that they love to listen, or (b) showing that they don't love to listen, or (c) neither?

1. Gary: "I know I'm right. I don't need to listen to you try to convince me that I'm not right."

2. Betty: "Jabber, jabber, jabber. You just talk and talk. Would you give a poor tired body like me some peace and quiet?"

3. Byron has been talking for half an hour, nonstop, to his co-worker Webster. He now says: "Web, I don't mean to monopolize our discussion. Do you have anything to say? But be quick, I've only got a few seconds."

4. Jerry: "This music is so loud that it's blowing out my eardrums. Could you turn it down a bit?"

5. Bill: "I'm plugging my ears. I don't want to hear another one of your critical statements about me."

6. Jim: "I need to stop listening to my friend Nat. I'm beginning to care too much about what he thinks. I'm a real man. I have a right to my own ideas. What do I care? I need to make my own decisions in life."

7. Patty: "I just have too many opinions, and I know I jabber on about them so much. My rate of learning slows each time my opinions get in the way. I need to just listen more and be more willing to accept other people's ideas."

Lesson 3

Opposing Viewpoints

When we are forming an opinion on an issue, it is often a good idea to collect other people's viewpoints on the issue. The more viewpoints we hear, the better we understand the whole picture.

EXAMPLE A

Oscar just knew he was right. He didn't need to read about all of those other viewpoints. Oscar knew they were all wrong. The group Oscar was with – called the Flat Earth Society – made sure its members knew why other positions were wrong. The International Headquarters published many little booklets which explained everything in simple language. Sometimes Oscar wondered how people could believe that the world was round – and not flat, as his group taught. Oscar figured that most people were just stupid and don't think about what they believe.

Dr. Weednut, a leading figure in the Flat Earth Society, had an entertaining way of explaining why society has deceived itself into believing that the earth is round, when everyone can see that it is obviously flat. Oscar liked Dr Weednut the first very time he met him. He stimulated Oscar to think, and he made thinking seem so easy. Oscar was glad he had someone whom he could trust to explain everything to him.

Oscar is not honestly evaluating both sides of the issue firsthand. He isn't studying things for himself. He has only listened to one side of the issue – the Flat Earth side. No wonder his side makes sense to him. Any side may seem logical if we only see things from that one point of view.

Many Counselors

"Where there is not guidance the people fall,
But in abundance of counselors there is victory."
Proverbs 11:14 (NASB)

In Proverbs, Solomon often counsels us to obtain advice from a wise man. But instead of obtaining advice from only one wise man, here Solomon directs us to gather advice from many wise men. Why is this?

If many people gave us their advice, but they all agreed with each other on everything, then we would learn nothing new. That's why we need to listen to advisors who disagree with each other. By hearing from a wide range of opinions, we are better able to choose the best advice (1 Corinthians 11:18-19).

EXAMPLE B

Wilby had a problem. He didn't know which brand of toothpaste to buy. He decided to try this new opposing viewpoints idea he'd been reading about in *The Fallacy Detective*. He decided to go around and ask different people what they thought.

Wendy (a store assistant who offered to help): "This type with 'Oxy-white Pro' is guaranteed to make your teeth whiter in twenty-four hours." (Wilby noticed that toothpaste brands with the 'Oxy-white Pro' sticker were twice the price of other brands.)

Phoebe (a friend of Wilby's): "Wilby, I think you'd have such a cute smile if you tried to get rid of some of those blueberry Popsicle stains in your mouth."

Judd (another friend): "Toothpaste? What's that? Real men don't brush their teeth."

Wilby's Mom: "Wilby, it really doesn't matter, as long as you don't buy anything that contains fluoride additives. You might come down with some terrible disease in a few years if you use fluoride."

Austin (Wilby's co-worker): "I only use Hug-A-Tree brand. It's made by a very environmentally conscious company from Denmark. And they promise that they don't test their products on whales."

Bob (who works out at the health club with Wilby): "I heard on a talk show that if you chew organic mint leaves, then your breath will smell good without having to brush your teeth."

Wilby concluded that he was worrying too much over nothing. He decided to keep using the brand of toothpaste he'd always used. It had always seemed to do the job. But now he understood more about how different people made their decisions.

We gain at least two benefits from looking at opposing viewpoints:
1. By studying new viewpoints, we gain the opportunity to change our own views if we are wrong. We would never have this opportunity if we only listened to things with which we agreed.
2. By studying new viewpoints, we can better help others. When we study a viewpoint which is wrong, we still learn many things. It helps us to understand how to defend our own views, and it helps us to communicate our views to others.

No one has the time to evaluate every viewpoint on every issue, but we all can be diligent to learn more about alternative views. This is another important part of having an *inquiring mind*.

Exercises

In the list of issues below, try to think of at least two sides to each issue. Some of these are well-known opposing viewpoints. If you think of a different pair of opposing viewpoints than we do in the Answer Key, that is all right. We have done the first one for you.

1. The Civil War – Example: the view of the Union, and the view of the Confederacy.

2. The reasons for the American Revolution.

3. Abortion.

4. The existence of God.

5. Homeschooling.

6. Breeds of dogs.

7. Gun control.

8. The origin of the universe and of life.

9. Slavery in America before 1860.

10. Logic.

11. Should little boys take baths?

12. Chicago baseball teams.

3

Avoiding the Question

PEANUTS reprinted by permission of United Feature Syndicate, Inc.

Lesson 4

Red Herring Fallacy

Consider the following conversation:

EXAMPLE A

Jenny: "Girls are much smarter than boys."
Bert: "Oh yeah. How do you know that?"
Jenny: "Because, they just are."
Bert: "But how do you know it?"
Jenny: "There are lots of girls who have done lots of smart things. Our neighbor, Mrs. Jones, is pretty smart; Joan of Arc saved the French from the English; and Madame Curie invented the light bulb."
Bert: "But how do you know they are smarter than boys?"
Jenny: "Because there are many girls who have high IQs. That makes them smart."
Bert: "You still haven't answered the question. Why are girls smarter than boys?"
Jenny: "Well, I'm smart and you're dumb. That proves it."

It should be clear that Jenny isn't really answering the question. She is saying things that sound like they answer the question, but they don't. She is trying to prove that girls are smarter than boys, but she is only showing that some girls are smart and saying nothing about how smart boys are.

It isn't that she is saying things that aren't true (except for the part about Madame Curie). But she isn't answering the real question of "why are girls smarter than boys?" If she were to really answer the question she could say something like:

Jenny: "Girls are smarter than boys because it has been proven that the average IQ of a girl is higher than the average IQ of a boy."

You see, when we argue, it can be difficult to stay on the topic – to answer the question we are arguing. It is easy to introduce something irrelevant into the argument. Also, it can be even more difficult to notice when somebody else is straying from the topic and introducing something irrelevant into the argument.

Whenever we introduce something irrelevant into an argument, we are *avoiding the question.*

Red Herring

When someone is avoiding the question and asserting something irrelevant, we say they are introducing a *red herring* into the argument. A red herring is a dead fish – a dead fish that has started to become "ripe" and smelly. Dog trainers used to use red herrings to train their tracking dogs. They would lay out a scent trail of a raccoon (or whatever they wanted the dog to learn to track) and let the trail become old, then they would drag the red herring (which, by this time, was very "ripe" and smelly) across the trail and off in a different direction. Then they would train the dogs to stay on the raccoon's scent trail and ignore the red herring's scent trail. So, a red herring is a distracting scent trail. In our context, a red herring is when someone brings up an irrelevant topic which distracts us from the real question.

A *red herring* **is the introduction of an irrelevant point into an argument. Someone may think (or they may want** *us* **to think) it proves his side, but it really doesn't.**

I am sure you have had this happen to you before: you are talking with somebody about something you disagree on and after a while you realize that you aren't discussing the thing you started out discussing. This is because, somewhere in the argument, somebody introduced a red herring and you have been arguing about the red herring ever since.

EXAMPLE B

> Jenny: "I think boys should always open doors for girls."
> Bert: "Why."
> Jenny: "Because, that is the gentlemanly thing to do."
> Bert: "Why is that the gentlemanly thing to do?"
> Jenny: "Because it is very helpful for the girls."
> Bert: "But wouldn't it also be a helpful thing for the boys if all the girls opened the doors for them? Why don't all the girls open the doors for the boys?"
> Jenny: "Because that isn't right. This afternoon, when we were coming out of the grocery store, I had several bags in my hands and I had to put them all down to open the door, just because you were too rude to help me."
> Bert: "I couldn't help you open the door because I was out in the parking lot waiting in the car."
> Jenny: "See what I mean? You were too inconsiderate to think that I might need some help when I came out of the grocery store. I think that was very ungentlemanly."
> Bert: "I didn't know that you were going to buy so many groceries, otherwise I would have."
> Jenny: "You should have thought of that."

Do you notice that Bert and Jenny aren't arguing anymore about whether boys should open doors for girls? Now, they are arguing about whether Bert should have opened the door for Jenny that afternoon. This is because Jenny introduced a red herring into the argument and Bert didn't notice. Bert should have said something like:

> Bert: "Maybe I should have opened the door for you today, but how does that show that boys should always open doors for girls?"

To properly answer the question, Jenny could have said:

> Jenny: "Because girls have smaller hands than boys so they can't turn door knobs as easily."

While there are some better arguments for why boys should open doors for girls, this one at least addresses the topic.

Calvin is introducing some red herrings here.
What he says has nothing to do with whether his dad should retrieve the ball.

Not a Red Herring

When somebody says "I don't know," and doesn't answer the question, he is not introducing a red herring. He is still addressing the topic – he just doesn't have an answer.

EXAMPLE C

Son: "What is the square root of 234.09667?"
Father: "I don't know. Why don't you go figure it out on a calculator?"

The father here is addressing his son's question. He just doesn't know the answer.

Exercises

In the following examples, is the speaker addressing the question and staying on topic? If he isn't, and he is introducing something irrelevant, shout "RED HERRING!" at the top of your lungs.

1. Son: "Why can't I go see the movie *The Day of the Spatulas* with my friends?"
   Dad: "Because it's a scary movie and you shouldn't see scary movies when you are this young."

2. Son: "Why can't I go see *The Day of the Spatulas* with my friends?"
   Dad: "Because January 1 falls on a Wednesday this year."

3. Son: "Why can't I go see *The Day of the Spatulas* with my friends?"
   Friend: "Because you don't have enough money for the ticket."

4. Son: "Why can't I go see *The Day of the Spatulas* with my friends?"
   Dad: "Isn't there some other kind of movie you could go to see instead?"

5. Son: "Dad, can I go see *The Day of the Spatulas* with my friends?
   Dad: "Why don't you go ask your mother?"

6. Son: "Dad, can I go see *The Day of the Spatulas* with my friends?
   Dad: "No."

7. Son: "Dad, can I go see *The Day of the Spatulas* with my friends?
   Dad: "I don't know. What is *The Day of the Spatulas*? Is it about pancakes?"

8. Son: "Dad, why did you go to see the movie *The Day of the Spatulas*, when you said I couldn't?"
   Dad: "It was a really good movie. I'll take you to see it next week."

Lesson 5

Recognizing Red Herrings

When someone introduces a red herring, he may be saying something which is true, although irrelevant.

EXAMPLE A

"Sparkledent is great for reducing cavities. Dentists say cavities are the number one dental problem in America."

This advertisement is saying something which is true: cavities are a big problem. However, it says nothing about how Sparkledent will reduce cavities. If the ad said something like: "Sparkledent is recommended by dentists everywhere as the number one cavity-reducing toothpaste, so you should use it," then it would be addressing the issue. Instead, it introduces a red herring.

Red herrings are often good arguments. The only problem is, they don't prove the point being argued – they prove something else.

EXAMPLE B

Son: "Spinach can't be good for me – it tastes terrible."

Mom: "It may taste terrible, but you still have to show me it isn't good for you."

It is often difficult to recognize when somebody is introducing a red herring. Here is an example which is a little harder to recognize. A tract from XYZ Ministries, titled *Ten Reasons to Believe in Life After Death*, gives the following as reason # 1:

EXAMPLE C

"The Injustices Of Life: It would be difficult to believe that life is good if we knew there was nothing beyond the grave to compensate for problems of inequality and unfairness. While some people seem destined for happiness, others are born into terrible relationships and circumstances. If we could be sure there was nothing to offset unequal distribution of suffering, many would have reason to curse the day of their birth for the way life has treated them (Job 3:1-3)."

If we summarized this, we might say: "We should believe in life after death because it would be unfair if there wasn't life after death." The author does make a good case that it would be very unpleasant if there wasn't an afterlife – if there wasn't, then the world would be pretty unfair. However, his argument does not show us that there is an afterlife. Therefore, this argument does not show us that we should believe in an afterlife – his argument is irrelevant. This idea is hard to grasp at first, until we remember that the only reason for anybody to believe in an afterlife (or anything else for that matter) is because there really is one – not because believing in it makes us feel good.

A much stronger argument for an afterlife would be to ask somebody who has already been there. We believe in life after death because Jesus has told us about it in the Bible. "I am the resurrection and the life. He who believes in Me, though he may die, he shall live" (John 11:25).

Exercises

A. In the following examples, answer these questions: (1) What is the question which is being argued over? (2) Is the speaker addressing the question and staying on topic? If he isn't, and he is introducing something irrelevant, scream "RED HERRING" at the top of your lungs.

1. "Grizzly bears can't be dangerous to humans – they look so cute."

2. "Why should I study math? I don't want to be a math teacher."

3. "People should make an effort to read a book a month, because reading a book will build their minds and their vocabulary. Building the mind and vocabulary is a good thing."

4. "I think that the government should raise taxes. It doesn't have enough money to spend on the programs which the American people need. The only way for the government to get enough money is to raise taxes."

5. "I think the government should lower taxes. The government is spending too much money on welfare programs. The people on welfare are ruining our economy by making us give our hard-earned money to them, when most of them could go out and get a job and earn it themselves. When people are on welfare, it lowers productivity and hurts the economy."

6. "Ten Reasons to Believe in Life After Death, Reason # 10 – Practical Effects: Belief in life after death is a source of personal security, optimism, and spiritual betterment (1 John 3:2). Nothing offers more courage than the confidence that there is a better life for those who use the present to prepare for eternity. Belief in the unlimited opportunities of eternity has enabled many to make the ultimate sacrifice of their own life on behalf of those they love." – A tract from XYZ Ministries.

7. When the presidential candidate was asked whether he'd name as a running mate someone who was opposed to abortion, he replied: "It would be incredibly presumptive for someone who has yet to earn his party's nomination to be picking a vice president. However, the main criterion I would use in choosing a running mate would be whether the person was capable of being president."

8. When the presidential candidate was asked whether he had ever used drugs he said: "No, I have never touched the stuff in my life."

9. When the presidential candidate was asked whether he had ever cheated on a test in school, he said: "I don't think that is any of your business. I don't think I have to answer questions like that, so I am not going to say."

10. "Now, some in Congress believe the national government has no business helping communities improve their schools....But I think strengthening education is a national priority." – Bill Clinton

11. "How can deforestation be so bad when there are so many uses for the wood?"

Lesson 6

Ad Hominem Attack

Now that we know how people use red herrings to avoid a question, we'll look at some of the different methods people use when they want to avoid a question.

One method is to attack the person making an argument instead of the argument itself. Let us look at a exchange which we hope never took place:

G. Washington: "I disagree with my distinguished opponent regarding his views on public housing for minorities. I think that it would be wrong for us to force the taxpayers to fund such an enterprise."

T. Jefferson: "I must insist that my opponent is mistaken in his beliefs, and the public should, in fact, disregard them. My reason is that he has been in the military most of his life and therefore he cannot have compassion for the feelings and needs of minorities."

G. Washington: "I must again disagree. My opinion is not influenced by my rank in life and my position in the military. My opponent, however, is not so clean from bias. His desire for public funding for housing for minorities stems from an unbalanced pity for them and his insane desire to further their cause. His opinion cannot be trusted."

T. Jefferson: "Whoa. We want to talk about biases, do we? What about your bigoted hatred for the Indians? If that doesn't influence your beliefs about minorities, then I don't know what would."

G. Washington: "My feelings about the Indians has nothing to do with this. But, as long as we are going to be insinuating things, I'm just wondering what you did on all of those trips to France? Nobody seems to know."

T. Jefferson: "What are *you* doing now? Attacking my character? Have I ever said anything about that cherry tree?"

Here, neither debater is conducting himself in a distinguished way. Neither of them is addressing his opponent's arguments. Instead, each is attacking his opponent's person. This is common in debates – especially political debates. If one debater can discredit his opponent's character or motives, then the public will often think badly of his opponent's argument as well. This is the *ad hominem* attack fallacy. "*Ad hominem*" is Latin for "to the man."

An *ad hominem* attack is attacking an opponent's character, or his motives for believing something, instead of disproving his argument.

EXAMPLE B

Jenny: "My uncle says that all murderers should be put to death because then nobody would want to murder anybody anymore."

Sylvia: "Wasn't your uncle in jail once? I don't think that we can trust somebody's opinion who was once a criminal."

This is not the right way to argue. Someone may have character flaws, but his argument can still be valid.

Charles Darwin, who developed the theory of evolution, also developed a different theory that is now almost universally accepted as true. It is called microevolution. Darwin noticed that a population of animals within a kind – say, finches – would, over time, change so that certain features would become more pronounced (the bill would become longer, to poke into deep holes; or the bill would become more curved to be able to do some other kind of thing). Darwin said that this was nature's way of adapting to changes in an environment. Microevolution is almost universally accepted today. However, Darwin then went on to theorize that animals (given enough time) could change so that they became a totally different animal – a monkey could evolve into a man. This is what we now call evolution (or macroevolution) and is hotly contested by Christians today.

Someone during Darwin's time could have said this about him:

EXAMPLE C

"We shouldn't believe in Darwin's theory of microevolution. He also believes that monkeys can turn into men."

This would be an irrelevant argument. This argument attacks Darwin's other beliefs, not the belief in question – microevolution. We need to take what Darwin says about microevolution and figure out whether he is right or wrong from that – ignoring his other beliefs on evolution. We should not throw out all his arguments just because he has some other bad ideas, or has a character flaw.

Ad hominem also occurs when somebody accuses his opponent of having bad motives.

EXAMPLE D

Jenny: "My uncle says that Robert E. Lee was a good, honest man."
Sylvia: "Doesn't your uncle come from Alabama? That's in the South. I don't think we need to give much weight to your uncle's arguments if he is from the South. He's obviously biased."

Jenny's uncle may be biased, but Sylvia shouldn't totally disregard his opinion because of that. A person's character or motives may influence his arguments, but these things don't necessarily have any bearing on the strength of his arguments.

Not *Ad Hominem*

It is *not* an *ad hominem* when someone only questions whether someone else is telling the truth.

EXAMPLE E

"I don't think we can trust Mr. Smith when he says that he was nowhere near the scene of the crime. He has been known to lie on many occasions, and he certainly has a motive for not telling the truth here."

The speaker here is not discrediting Mr. Smith's *opinion* by saying he has a bad character. He is discrediting Mr. Smith's ability *to state the facts* – he can't be trusted to tell the truth.

Exercises

What form of bad reasoning, if any, do you find in the following exercises?

1. "Senator Ribbet is a liar. You shouldn't listen to his opinion on anything."

2. "Senator Ribbet is a liar. You can't believe him when he tells you something."

3. "I know everybody thinks Einstein's theory of relativity is correct, but I can't accept it. Einstein believed in evolution."

4. "We all know Senator Ribbet's view on abortion. But what about that incident where he got drunk, crashed his car, and ended up killing somebody? In light of that, how can we listen to his views?"

5. "I never met a man I didn't like."

6. "Mr. Jones has some good-sounding ideas. His idea of reducing costs while increasing output sounds promising. However, did you know that Mr. Jones was an alcoholic before he came to work with us?"

7. Mom: "Did you take out the trash, Bert?"
   Bert: "Why are you always suspecting me of things?"

8. Mrs. A: "I'm going through a logic book with my kids. It's called *The Fallacy Detective*. I really like it."
   Mrs. B: "Aw, the authors of that book are just a bunch of homeschoolers. What do they know about logic?"

9. Distinguished Senator A: "I am in favor of the federal government building a dam over the Watchichokiehatchie River. I think it would help agriculture in the region, which would benefit this country's economy greatly."
Distinguished Senator B: "That is fine for you to say. The Watchichokiehatchie River is located in your state, and if this bill goes through and the dam is built, then you will probably be reelected next term."

10. Bert: "I heard that Joseph Stalin was an evil, cruel man who stopped at nothing to gain power over Europe during WWII."
Jenny: "What! Without the help of Stalin, we couldn't have beaten the Germans."

11. "My cousin says he is getting a real race car for his birthday. He says it can go 298 miles per hour. I don't believe him. He lies about everything."

12. Jenny: "The American Revolution was one of the highest points in American history. In that time period, great strides were taken in the development of government."
Clyde: "Naw, it wasn't. I heard George Washington was a Mason."

Lesson 7

Genetic Fallacy

The genetic fallacy is another personal attack fallacy. It is called "genetic" because it addresses the genesis, or beginning, of something. The genetic fallacy is different from *ad hominem* because it does not attack the person making the argument. It attacks the place where the argument came from.

> The *genetic fallacy* is condemning an argument because of where it began, how it began, or who began it.

EXAMPLE A

Jenny: "I think abortion is the murder of innocent children."
Clyde: "Ah. The only reason why you disagree with abortion is because you were abused as a child and have never gotten over it."

It is very difficult to argue with somebody when he uses this fallacy. No matter what you say, he will just claim you are saying it because of your difficult past, and therefore, everybody can ignore what you say.

It seems that people think that if an idea came out of the Russian Revolution, or was first proposed by a pagan man, then it has to be bad. The idea may be bad, but it is not *necessarily* bad because of the source. If an argument was made up by a bad person or came out of a bad historical event, it doesn't mean the argument is bad itself.

EXAMPLE B

"[We need to question whether the person who won the electoral college vote – but didn't get the popular vote – should become president, because] …the electoral college was invented largely as a scheme to allow southern states to count slaves as three-fifths human, insuring their domination of national elections for the first decades of the Republic." — Jesse Jackson

The electoral college (which is the system the Constitution laid out for choosing the president) may have been created by people with bad motives, but that doesn't necessarily make the electoral college bad *now*. Many factors may have changed since then.

EXAMPLE C

Bert: "Mr. Gritchus, why do you always wear suspenders and never a belt?"

Mr. Gritchus: "Because belts were developed in the military centuries ago and were used by soldiers. Since the military is evil, and belts came from the military, therefore I can't wear a belt."

Even if belts did come out of the military – which Mr. Gritchus thinks is evil – that fact doesn't mean that if Mr. Gritchus wears one, then he is *in* the military and participating in their evil. He may still wear them for good reasons – like holding up his pants – sinlessly.

Exercises

What form of bad reasoning, if any, do you find in the following exercises?

1. "You can tell a lot about a fellow's character by his way of eating jelly beans." – Ronald Reagan

2. "Good grief! You're thirty-five years old and you still believe in Santa Claus? You only believe that because you fell down a well when you were three and haven't recovered since."

3. "You disagree with the idea of women in the military just because of your Baptist upbringing."

4. Bert: "This encyclopedia says Columbus discovered America in 1492."
   Jenny: "The one I have here says he discovered America in 1924. How many volumes are in your encyclopedia?"
   Bert: "Four."
   Jenny: "Well, that proves it. Mine has 18. Mine must be right."

5. "Taking drugs can't be bad. There are lots of people who enjoy it."

6. "Our earliest human ancestors had fears. They had fears of accidents happening to them, of becoming sick and dying, and being harmed by rival tribes. As a result, certain persons within a tribe would claim they had powers to protect others from these dangers. They had certain spells and incantations which, they said, would protect people from harm. This belief, over the course of history, developed into the belief in gods. I see no reason to believe there is a God, since this belief only came from our desires to stop worrying."

7. Bert: "I've been reading this really good book called *The Fallacy Detective*. It's about recognizing bad reasoning."
   Sylvia: "You're reading that book? Isn't that book about logic? Logic is evil. Logic came out of ancient Greece and ancient Greece was pagan. The first person we know about who talked about logic was Aristotle, and he was a pagan."

8. "I think I heard that the famous author, O. Henry, was in prison once. I don't think I'm going to read any more of his books."

9. "The fashions in London come straight from Paris, and the fashions in Paris come straight from Hades."

10. "Senator A has given us reasons for increasing the pay for military personnel. But we all know that Senator A has three sons who are in the military, so his family would benefit greatly if their pay was increased."

Lesson 8

Tu Quoque

Tu quoque means in Latin "you too."

Tu quoque is dismissing someone's viewpoint on an issue because he himself is inconsistent in that very thing.

EXAMPLE A

Fred: "I wouldn't smoke cigarettes if I were you. It is a bad habit and it will bring you all kinds of problems."
Jake: "Don't tell me not to smoke. You do it, too."

Jake's comment is irrelevant to Fred's concerns – smoking is still bad for Jake. Fred might have some very good reasons for telling Jake to not smoke cigarettes. He may have begun smoking when he was young, and now he can't stop. Fred may not want to see Jake ruin his life like Fred did.

People who commit this fallacy often have guilty consciences, and it makes them feel better somehow when they shift their guilt onto someone else.

EXAMPLE B

"I don't see what is wrong with the Spanish bullfight. I enjoy watching it myself. I know a lot of people say it is cruel and unmercifully violent. But look at the kinds of sports you Americans enjoy: boxing – where two people beat each other up until one falls down, and football – where two teams tackle each other and a whole team piles up on one man. And what about your violent movies? You watch violent movies where people are killed and dismembered right before your very eyes."

This man doesn't address the point: is the Spanish bullfight cruel? He hopes to shift attention onto everybody else's sins.

This fallacy also happens when somebody claims that two wrongs make a right.

EXAMPLE C

"I don't see what is wrong with speeding. Everybody does it."

Of course, the point is not whether everybody does it, but whether it is right. If everybody else is risking their lives and breaking the law, that doesn't give you a right to do it, too.

Exercises

What form of bad reasoning, if any, do you find in the following exercises?

1. "I don't see what right you have to question where I get my money for my campaigns. Wasn't it you, four years ago, who became entangled in a big scandal where 23 congressmen were caught laundering money through the congressional post office?"

2. "While [Jesse] Jackson emphasized from the start that the dispute [over whether to allow several black youths back in school, after they had caused a fight] was about 'fairness' and not race, some of the protesters Sunday ... noted that all of the board members who voted to expel the students were white and the only dissenting vote was from a black member..."

3. "That church cannot possibly be good. It was formed by an unregenerate heretic."

4. "My opponent cannot be trusted when he says he has had no illegal contributions to his campaign. Last term, he was caught lying on several occasions."

5. In response to someone's comment that the military is overcommitted and underresourced and worse off today than it was eight years ago, Senator Joseph Lieberman said, "Most important, I want to assure the American people the American military is the best-trained, best-equipped, most powerful force in the world, and that Al Gore and I will do whatever it takes to keep them that way."

6. "Only those who are chronically obese would oppose dietary restrictions."

7. "It's okay to walk on Mr. Jones's property without asking him. Last week, when I was over here, I met a bunch of boys in the orchard eating apples. People walk on Mr. Jones's land all the time without asking him."

8. "O. J. Simpson couldn't have murdered his wife. He's in the Pro Football Hall of Fame. He's famous!"

9. Jenny: "I think all wars are evil. They are just about killing, and we shouldn't get involved with them."
Bert: "Do you think war is wrong even if our country is being invaded?"
Jenny: "That's impossible. Our country will never be invaded. We are friends with Canada, Mexico would never think of it, and nobody could go all the way across the ocean."
Bert: "Ah, but you're wrong there, our country was invaded in 1941 when Pearl Harbor was attacked."
Jenny: "But Pearl Harbor was a naval base at that time, and not a state."

10. "I hear all these environmentalists talking about how we should save the environment and all that. It seems kind of ridiculous to me. These same people go to the grocery store and put their groceries in plastic bags, they have houses made out of wood, and they drive gas-guzzling cars. I think they're ridiculous."

11. "I think Joseph Stalin was a dirty rotten scoundrel. I heard that he murdered his wife. It wouldn't surprise me, from what other things I have heard about him."

Lesson 9

Faulty Appeal to Authority

When we aren't knowledgeable on a certain subject, the wise thing is to ask an authority – somebody who is knowledgeable on the subject.

EXAMPLE A

You: "My car won't run. What's wrong with it?"

Mechanic: "Hmmmm.... It looks like you have a broken timing chain, warped camshaft, and the U-Joints are shot. That will have to be fixed before it will run."

You do what the mechanic says because he knows more about cars than you do, and you don't want to take the time to learn. The mechanic is the authority, and you trust him. We all do this every day without thinking about it. When we want to know how high Mount McKinley is, we don't take a yardstick and climb up 20,320 feet to find out. We look it up in a book. We trust that book because the authors have been to Mount McKinley and we haven't. They are authorities on the subject. An *authority* is someone who has special knowledge on a particular subject.

EXAMPLE B

Prosecuting Attorney: "Mrs. Jones, were you there when your husband was murdered?"

Mrs. Jones: "Yes."

Prosecuting Attorney: "And who was the murderer?"

Mrs. Jones: "That man right there."

Mrs. Jones is an authority on the subject of what happened at the murder scene because she was there.

We are *appealing to an authority* when we claim something is true because an authority said it was true. Appealing to the advice of an authority can be good when we do it in the right way. However, if the person we are appealing to is not actually an authority in the area we are discussing, our appeal is faulty.

EXAMPLE C

"My car mechanic says the best way to fix computer problems is to just give the computer a good, sharp kick. He says it should always work."

Your car mechanic may be knowledgeable when working with cars, but it is not likely he has any special knowledge about computers. We should not appeal to him as an authority on computers.

A *faulty appeal to authority* **is an appeal to someone who has no special knowledge in the area being discussed.**

Unfortunately, some people use an appeal to authority in the wrong way. They appeal to an authority when arguing with people just to overawe them.

EXAMPLE D

Bert: "I've been homeschooled all of my life, and I think it has helped me a lot."

Clyde: "You think so, huh? I was just reading in a magazine where they interviewed the man who has the highest IQ in the world. This man said he didn't think homeschooling turned out good citizens. He said he didn't think homeschoolers received enough socialization, so they will become social misfits. Do you still think homeschooling is a good idea?"

Bert: "That sounds bad … especially if that man is the smartest person in the world. He must know plenty. Maybe homeschooling didn't help me as much as I thought."

Clyde is using a faulty appeal to authority against Bert. Bert is being over-awed by the intelligence of the man with the highest IQ in the world. If Bert thought about it a little more, he would realize that the smartest man in the world may be good at logic problems, and he may be able to beat anybody at Scrabble or chess, but that doesn't mean he knows anything about the effects of homeschooling on children.

When someone uses an appeal to authority as a way to overawe us and make us reluctant to challenge that authority's viewpoint, he is committing a *faulty appeal to authority.*

Movie stars are often used in faulty appeals to authority.

EXAMPLE E

"If Paul Newman thinks organic foods are more nutritious than chemical-saturated foods, shouldn't you, too?"

We have no reason to think Paul Newman is an authority on nutrition. If someone is a respected authority on one subject – such as acting – we tend to think he will also be an authority in other areas – like nutrition. Nobody wants to contradict a movie star, especially if he's good-looking.

When the topic under discussion is controversial among respected authorities, then appealing simply to the opinion of a single authority is a *faulty appeal to authority.*

If many accepted authorities disagree on a particular subject, we can't say *our* favorite authority is the correct one – there may be many other equally respected authorities who disagree.

EXAMPLE F

Bert: "I've been homeschooled all of my life, and I think it has helped me a lot."
Clyde: "Not according to the president of the National Education Association. He says homeschooling stunts a child's social, moral, and academic development, and it turns a kid into a geeky nerd. You must believe the president of the National Education Association. He is a respected authority on the subject of education."

Bert: "That's funny, the president of the National Homeschooling Association says homeschooling produces people who are intelligent, socially adaptable, and bring great benefits to society. He also says that public school students often turn into social troublemakers. You must believe the president of the National Homeschooling Association. He is a very respected authority on education."

Homeschooling is a controversial topic among educators of all types. Neither Clyde nor Bert can say homeschooling is good or bad just because a particular authority on education said so. They need to prove their sides in other ways, such as statistical evidence.

Exercises

A. Which of the following appeals to authority are good and which ones are faulty?

1. Prosecuting Attorney: "In relation to the scene of the crime, where were you at the time of the murder?"
   Witness: "I was two blocks away, mowing my lawn."
   Prosecuting Attorney: "And what did you see?"
   Witness: "I heard what sounded like a gunshot, so I looked up and I saw the defendant running away from where the murder was committed. I figured he must have murdered someone, so I tackled him and called the cops."
   Prosecuting Attorney: "See, there you have it, straight from a man who was there at the scene of the crime. He says this man is guilty."

2. Defense Attorney: "What is your relationship to my client?"
   Witness: "I cut his hair about once a month when he comes in to my barber shop."
   Defense Attorney: "And do you think this man is capable of murder?"
   Witness: "No, he seemed like a mild-mannered guy to me."
   Defense Attorney: "There you have it, straight from someone who knows him. My client is not capable of committing this heinous crime."

3. Defense Attorney: "What is your relationship to my client?"
   Witness: "I am his wife."
   Defense Attorney: "And, would you consider him capable of murder?"
   Witness: "He couldn't squash a mosquito if it was biting him; he's that mild-mannered."
   Defense Attorney: "There you have it, this man's wife says he is not capable of murder."

4. You: "I'm having trouble playing my violin here. Do you have any suggestions?"
   Mechanic: "Maybe if you blow in the other end instead?"

5. You: "I'm having trouble playing my violin here. Do you have any suggestions?"
   Violin Teacher: "Hmmmm.... I can see why you are having trouble. That isn't a violin. It's a bassoon."

6. "My uncle says you shouldn't spank kids when they are bad. He says it stunts their growth."

7. "I'm not ever going to buy a Ford. My mechanic says they break down easily. He says all the other mechanics agree with him."

8. Doctor: "Take two pills and call me in the morning."
   Patient: "Why?"
   Doctor: "Because I think it will be good for you."

B. What form of bad reasoning, if any, do you find in the following exercises?

9. "Have your face lifted at Acme Cosmetic Surgery. If you want to know how good people look after we're done with them, just ask Elizabeth Taylor."

10. Judge: "Mr. Jones, can you explain to me why you broke all your neighbor's windows?
    Accused: "They were playing loud polka music. I hate polka music."
    Judge: "Didn't you know that was wrong?"
    Accused: "You can argue with me about this all you want. I don't think it will change anything. I heard some obnoxious music coming out of their house, so I took action. Playing loud music in town is against the law, isn't it? Unless you can come up with some evidence which contradicts that, I don't think you have much of a case against me."

11. "I think scientists are wrong. There is no such thing as global warming. I just finished talking to my boss and he thought the idea was ridiculous."

12. "This book called *The Fallacy Detective* says it is a fallacy to appeal to somebody who isn't an authority on any subject. This book must be right because the authors sure know plenty about logical thinking."

13. "I don't think we need to bother listening to your views on this. We all know you are just one of those hyper-liberals."

Lesson 10

Appeal to the People

Person Calling Phone Company: "I heard that you are now charging us for local calls. I am calling to complain. You have no right to charge us for that – you are making enough money as it is. You are the only phone company around here, so you think you can get away with highway robbery."

Phone Company: "I hear what you are saying and appreciate your openness on these issues."

Person: "I don't want you to appreciate anything. I don't want to pay for local calls."

Phone Company: "You see, when we were discussing this issue, it came to our attention that it is now common in this nation to pay for local calls. In fact the people over in the next state are paying for them now."

Person: "So?"

Phone Company: "Did you know that the people in most European countries have been paying for local calls for years?"

Person: "So?"

Phone Company: "It's funny that you have been the only person to call and complain about this new policy. Everybody else seems to be taking it just fine."

Person: "So?"

Phone Company: "Thank you for your input.... Click..."

The phone company is not addressing the caller's arguments. The phone company is bringing up irrelevant topics. It is irrelevant that people in the U.S. commonly pay for local calls. It is irrelevant that Europe has been paying for them. And it is just as irrelevant that the caller is the only person to complain about the new policy. The phone company is avoiding the question. The phone company is committing the fallacy of *appeal to the people*.

When we claim that our viewpoint is correct because many other people agree with it, we are committing the *appeal to the people* fallacy.

This fallacy is very similar to the faulty appeal to authority. If it is wrong to appeal to someone who isn't an authority, then it is just as wrong to appeal to many people who are not authorities. The general public is rarely a proper authority on any subject.

EXAMPLE B

Political Candidate: "My opponent says abortion is murder – despite the fact that a recent poll concluded 76% of Americans believe an abortion does not murder an innocent child."

Murder is still murder, whether or not many persons permit it to happen. The politician should do what is right, no matter what the public thinks. The general public is not an authority on what is moral or what is immoral. This is an appeal to the people.

EXAMPLE C

"This new book, *The Fallacy Detective*, must be the best logic book around. It has been on the best-seller list for months."

We should all know that the most popular book isn't necessarily the best book. This is an appeal to the people.

EXAMPLE D

"It looks as if more people vacation in Florida than any other place. It must be the nicest place in America to visit."

If more people vacation in Florida, then we might be able to say it is *a nice* place to visit. But, we can't say it is *the nicest* place to visit. People might vacation in Florida because it is cheaper – although they really want to go to Hawaii.

This fallacy is covered again in the chapter on *Propaganda*, under the title *bandwagon*.

Exercises

What form of bad reasoning, if any, do you find in the following exercises?

1. Jenny: "I'm worried about the economy. I think we are entering a depression."
   Bert: "I wouldn't worry. I heard that 89% of Americans believe the economy is improving."

2. Clyde: "I believe in reincarnation."
   Jenny: "Why would you believe in reincarnation."
   Clyde: "Shirley MacLaine is very famous, and she has written many books on the subject, and she believes in it."

3. Clyde: "I believe in reincarnation."
   Jenny: "Why would you believe in reincarnation."
   Clyde: "Shirley MacLaine is very famous and has written many books on the subject. She wouldn't have sold any copies if it wasn't true."

4. Jenny: "What's the capital of South Dakota?"
   Bert: "The guy at the library said it was Tulsa, but I wouldn't believe him. It didn't look like he worked there."

5. "What! You're telling me to go on a diet? What about you? You're seventy-five pounds overweight."

6. "My uncle is a child psychologist and pediatrician. He says you shouldn't spank children when they are bad. He says it stunts their growth."

7. "We need to give a large subsidy to farmers. The price of corn is so low right now that farmers are going broke. They are being forced to sell their land to pay for their debts. If this keeps up, most of the small, family-owned farms will disappear and we will be left with only large factory farms."

8. "Every developed nation in the world has strict controls on firearms, except America."

9. "Everybody's buying these new llama wool coats. They must be warm."

10. "This song has been on the top of the charts for over a month. It must be a very popular song."

Lesson 11

Straw Man

The fallacy of *straw man* is changing or exaggerating an opponent's position or argument to make it easier to refute.

EXAMPLE A

Mother to son: "I think you have been playing too many of those video games lately. I don't think they stimulate your mind as much as other activities would."

Son: "Oh, so you think I should just throw away the $1,000 video game collection I have and sit up in my room practicing IQ tests all day?"

This is not what the mother said. The son is exaggerating his mother's viewpoint. She thought he should play fewer video games – not no video games at all. The son committed the straw man fallacy.

The straw man fallacy distorts an opponent's position just enough to make it weak. The new argument that is created is called a "straw man" because it is easy to knock down. ("I'll huff and I'll puff and I'll blow your argument down.") The original argument was not nearly as easy to knock down.

EXAMPLE B

Political Candidate A: "Due to this year's budget problems, I think our state should decrease the amount of money going to the schools. This would solve the problem. We could bring the amount of money back to normal next year."

Political Candidate B: "My fellow citizens of this state. Is this what you want in a candidate? Someone who is against our schools, against our children's education, and against our future?"

Candidate B created a straw man argument, then attacked it. Candidate A only wanted to spend less money on the schools for one year, but Candidate B distorted this to mean Candidate A was against all education. It is much easier to refute someone who is against all education than it is to refute someone who wants something much more mild, such as decreasing spending on schools for one year.

EXAMPLE C

Clyde: "I don't think the North had any right to invade the South during the Civil War."

Sylvia: "I can't believe you said that. Slavery was cruel and brutal. Saying the slaves should have been ignored is wrong. The slaves should have been freed immediately."

Clyde is not saying that the slaves should not have been freed immediately. He is only saying that it was not the job of the North to invade the South. Sylvia is distorting Clyde's viewpoint. She is creating a straw man argument.

EXAMPLE D

Parent to daughter: "Your mother and I have decided that we don't want you to date when you are this young. And when you are old enough, we believe there should be some parental supervision."

Daughter: "Oh, now I understand. You're going to make me sit up in my room all my life until you pick out somebody for me to marry."

Children should not assume the worst about their parents' beliefs. They should take the time to find out exactly what they mean by what they say.

The straw man fallacy is similar to the red herring fallacy. A straw man argument introduces an irrelevant position – a position which nobody in the argument really believes in – then attacks it.

DILBERT reprinted by permission of United Feature Syndicate, Inc.

Tina is committing a straw man fallacy. She is distorting what Dogbert said.

Exercises

What form of bad reasoning, if any, do you find in the following exercises?

1. Bert: "I've been learning about the Second World War lately. I found out that America provoked Japan into attacking Pearl Harbor. I don't think that was the right thing for us to do. Jenny: "Oh, so you are now taking the side of the Axis? Do you think Germany and Japan were right to do what they did?

2. "This new book, *The Fallacy Detective*, must be a very popular book. It has been on the best-seller list for months."

3. "Recent polls indicate that millions of Americans are now concerned that global warming will put Los Angeles under water in 20 years. Shouldn't you be concerned also?"

4. When a midwestern state's Board of Education voted to embrace new standards for science textbooks, standards which did not include evolution as a scientific principle (making teaching it optional), the presidents of six public universities wrote a letter to the Board of Education. The letter said: "We are horrified at what you are doing to education in this state. This will set our state back a century. When the science teachers in this state hear about this, they will consider pursuing their career fields in states which are less prone to censoring science."

5. "Nearly everyone I know thinks Clyde is a liar."

6. "The Supreme Court right now is deciding whether it is right to execute insane people who have committed murder. I think it is all right to execute insane people. If we ban executions of insane people, then everybody on death row will suddenly decide they are insane and purposely fail sanity tests. It would result in chaos."

7. Mrs.: "Our car isn't running right. I think we need to buy a better one – something more comfortable."
Mr.: "Oh, so you want us to buy a brand new fancy car? I don't think we have enough money for a Rolls Royce."

8. "There can't be any global warming going on. I've asked about ten people today whether they thought there was global warming, and they all said there probably wasn't."

9. "Religion is a bunch of baloney. It all comes from chemical reactions in the brain."

10. Man on the Street: "I'm opposed to capital punishment."
Man on the Sidewalk: "Oh, you people who oppose punishing criminals make me sick. Don't you ever think about the poor victims at all?"

11. "The local talk show host said yesterday that we are on the verge of nuclear war. I think I'm going to sit in my basement for the next couple of weeks."

12. "I wouldn't worry about a little cheating on Tuesday's test if I were you. The test format makes it so easy for you to do a little cribbing, and everybody else does it."

Making Assumptions

Lesson 12

The Story of Aroup Goupta

Read the following story about Aroup Goupta very carefully. (You must roll the "r" to pronounce the name "Aroup" correctly.) Assume that what is said in this story is all true, and that no one in the story is lying or saying anything which is false. At the end of the story, we will ask you some questions about the story. In your answers, you must stick to what you know was literally said in the story, not what you think was meant.

THE STORY OF AROUP GOUPTA

The cat sat there wide-eyed and speechless – as much as a cat can be speechless – for a moment, and then bounded away.

Aroup continued to the end of the alley and turned left. He was now in the most densely populated part of the capital city. He was in a marketplace, and vendor stalls ran along both sides of the street. Aroup heard a vendor chanting in a singsong, "Beets. Fresh beets. Fresh beets for sale."

Aroup was hungry. But he had only two papushkas – the currency used in Clovnia – in his pocket. He did not have enough to buy any food.

"Which way is the center of town?" Aroup asked the dusty looking vendor.

The man looked up and motioned with his arm. "Down zat vay," he said.

Aroup continued down the street. He wondered, again, where he would stay the night. "Lief is a cursed city in a cursed country," he muttered to himself.

It was now growing hotter, and Aroup was forced to take off his woolen sweater. As he did so, Aroup glanced to his left. A man with a large bushy moustache was motioning to him from a doorway.

"Come here. I am a friend," the man said. He motioned again, urgently.

Aroup went over to him. He remembered he must be careful to whom he talked. The man grabbed Aroup by the shoulders and whispered in his ear, "My life and yours are not vorth a plug papushka if vee are seen. Hurry," he said and pulled Aroup through the door.

The room Aroup entered was very dimly lit, compared with the outside. "Hurry," the man said again, and this time he pulled up a chair next to a booth and pushed Aroup into it. "I vill bring you oatmeal."

As his eyes became accustomed to the dark, Aroup saw that he was in a restaurant. The ceiling was low, and the room smelled of mothballs and stale pipe tobacco. In the center of the room, a dozen short men were clustered around a table, drinking beet juice.

Presently, the man with the moustache returned carrying a plate of cold oatmeal. "You must eat zis slowly," he said. "Tonight you vill stay here."

Aroup obliged, for he was very hungry. The oatmeal, though it was cold and tasted terrible, was good in his stomach.

The man with the moustache sat down next to him and said something that must have been in the Cloveneeze language. "Oum av humby av a fpup pib," the man said.

"What was that?" Aroup said. "Are you a native Clovnian?"

"Only native Clovnians can speak Cloveneeze," the man said in English. "It vas very hard to find you. Have you been here long, Aroup Goupta?"

"No," Aroup responded. "I came here yesterday."

"Then you do not know the news?"

Aroup had heard no news since arriving.

What the news was, the little man with the moustache never said, for at that very moment the doors burst open and several tall men in uniforms strode in, brandishing clubs.

A tall, uniformed man, evidently the leader of the group, strode into the middle of the room and removed a Popsicle from his mouth.

"Ver is de sympathizers?" he said. He spoke not in the common Cloveneeze, but the more coarse French.

All the short men at the table froze for a moment and then rushed for the door.

Aroup was on his feet, and was about to follow the short men to the door, when he felt something on his arm. He looked over, not to see the man with the moustache, but a tall woman.

"Follow me," she said, and led him out a door at the back of the room.

"Here," the woman said, "take this." She handed Aroup a cat. "You must go through those doors. Behind them is an alley. Go down the alley until you are out of sight." The woman gave him a push and disappeared.

Aroup opened the doors and walked through, clutching the cat. He found himself in the dark alley. He stood there for a moment, wondering what to do. "I wish this all was just a bad dream." The cat hissed, and Aroup dropped it on the ground. His put his sweater back on.

The cat sat there wide-eyed and speechless – as much as a cat can be speechless – for a moment, and then bounded away.

Aroup continued to the end of the alley and turned left. He was now in the most densely populated part of the capital city. He was in a marketplace, and vendor stalls ran along both sides of the street. Aroup heard a vendor chanting in a singsong, "Beets. Fresh beets. Fresh beets for sale...."

Exercises

Read the following statements, and indicate whether (a) you think the statement is true, or (b) you don't know if the statement is true. In your answers, stick to what you know was said in the story. As you answer each exercise, check your answer. You can look back at the story if you need to.

1. Aroup Goupta was a man, not a woman.

2. Aroup was in a city.

3. Aroup was in a capital city.

4. Aroup was in a country called Clovnia.

5. Aroup was in the most densely populated part of the city.

6. Aroup was probably a foreign journalist come to investigate the political unrest in the country.

7. Aroup had a sweater with him.

8. Aroup was over twenty-five years old.

9. The man with the moustache was Aroup's friend.

10. The man with the moustache pulled Aroup into a restaurant.

11. The man with the moustache spoke Cloveneeze.

12. The man with the moustache was a native Clovnian.

13. The man with the moustache could have worked at the restaurant.

14. The short men were drinking beet juice.

15. The leader of the uniformed men wanted to know where the sympathizers were.

16. The short men at the table were afraid of being arrested as "sympathizers."

17. Aroup thought the oatmeal tasted terrible.

18. Aroup ate the oatmeal.

19. Aroup was too young to be in a restaurant where they served beet juice.

20. The tall woman wanted to save Aroup.

21. Aroup escaped in the nick of time.

22. This is the story that never ends.

Lesson 13

Assumptions

In the previous lesson, we told you the story of Aroup Goupta, then we asked you questions about the story. You may have given wrong answers to some of the exercises because you thought the story said something which it actually did not say. This lesson aims to show you the value of being aware of your assumptions.

Which Letter Is Different?

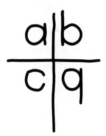

In the diagram above, which of the alphabet letters is different from all the others? (Note the letter which looks like a "9" is actually a lower case "Q.")

"a" This letter is different in that it is the first letter of the alphabet. It is the only letter made with a short stem on the right. It is the only vowel.

"b" This letter is different in that it is the only letter with a stem on the left of the circle, not on the right. It is the only letter made with its stem pointing upwards.

"c" This letter is different in that it is the only letter with a break in its circle instead of a stem. It is the only letter which is made of only one part.

"q" This letter is different in that it is the only letter which does not follow the others in alphabetical order. It is the only one which is made with its stem pointing downwards.

Do you think that we could make an argument for each individual letter being more different than the others? Is there something you are missing about this picture? Have our questions influenced you to make an assumption which is not true?

What about the "t" in the middle? It is larger than all the others. It is in the center of the diagram. It is made with two straight lines and no curved part. Did you forget about this letter?

Did the questions we asked about the diagram cause you to ignore an obvious part of the diagram? Assumptions can be dangerous things when we are not aware of them.

(We are grateful to David Pratt for the preceding illustration.)

EXAMPLE A

At the County Fair, there was a line of stalls displaying all the champion farm animals. One afternoon, during the fair, a man wearing a black vest walked up to the prize Jersey cow, shot her, and then ran out of the display barn. Even though there was a crowd of people around, no one tried to follow the man in the vest. Why was this?

EXAMPLE B

Dr. Taylor lives in Chicago. He had a speaking engagement in St. Louis. He and his wife drove there in the morning. When the lecture was over that evening, they got in their car and continued to drive in the same direction which they had driven earlier that day. They returned home that night, about six hours after leaving the lecture hall. How can this be?

We will tell you the answers to these riddles soon. Be patient.

Being Aware

An *assumption* is something taken for granted, or accepted as true without proof.

This whole chapter – especially this lesson – is about how people make assumptions without being aware of them. When two people argue, they may have different assumptions. If they knew what they were assuming, then they might realize why they were wrong, or why they both did not actually disagree.

To be aware of assumptions, you need to learn a healthy sense of suspicion – suspicion of everybody, including yourself. If someone is deceived, he is thoroughly convinced that he is not deceived – he does not know what his assumptions are. How can we make ourselves aware of all our assumptions? We can't. No one can be totally objective. We can only try to be as objective as we can.

Here are three suggestions on how to be objective:

1. Listen. Every time we listen to someone else's viewpoint, we give ourselves the opportunity to become un-deceived.

2. Evaluate our assumptions. It is important to recognize that everyone has a bias, and that we need to understand and to manage our own biases. We need to be aware of the assumptions which we are making. Keep asking, "Why do I think this is true?" There is nothing wrong with having assumptions, just as long as we have the correct assumptions.

3. Evaluate other people's assumptions. We should be alert to clues in what people say which may indicate their assumptions. This will give us insight into why they believe what they believe.

Answers

Example A: The man shot the Jersey cow with his camera. He was a journalist for the county newspaper, and he was in a hurry because he had a deadline. Did you have assumptions about what "shot" meant? Did you interpret "shot" to mean that the man in the vest killed the Jersey cow?

Example B: Dr. Taylor lives in Chicago, but he did not leave for the lecture from Chicago. He was staying south of St. Louis that morning, and he and his wife drove north to St. Louis to his speaking engagement. Afterwards they continued driving north to Chicago, which is about six hours from St. Louis. Did you assume that when we said that Dr. Taylor lived in Chicago that he started his drive from Chicago? Be careful of those nasty little assumptions!

Exercises

A. Brent: "Mom, if you buy that expensive toaster, we won't be able to go out for ice cream after lunch. It's my birthday, and I want to have ice cream."

Based on the paragraph above Brent is probably assuming which of the following:

1. There is a limited supply of money in his Mom's purse.
2. He gets to have what he wants on his birthday.
3. All toasters are expensive.
4. There is no such thing as free ice cream.
5. His Mom didn't buy ice cream for him the day before and put it in the freezer.
6. Ice cream melts when you put it in a toaster.

B. Answer the following riddles. See if you can catch the hidden assumptions.

7. Mrs. White, the housekeeper, swept the Blackhurst mansion. She swept all the dust and dirt in the rooms into five different piles around the house – two upstairs and three downstairs. Then she asked Bidwell, the butler, to help her sweep all the piles together. How many piles of dust will they have?

8. Why are 1996 U.S. pennies worth more than 1967 U.S. pennies?

9. Answer each of these riddle questions, then check your answers at the end:

a. What color is snow?

b. What color is the opposite of black?

c. What color is a boiled egg if you take out the yolk?

d. What color are most clouds on a peaceful summer's day?

e. What color is the largest part of people's eyes?

f. What color is the paper this is printed on?

g. What color are most clothes when you bleach them?

h. What color of cloth commonly keeps you the coolest in the hot sun?

i. What do cows drink?

Lesson 14

Circular Reasoning

An argument which says "P is true because Q is true, and Q is true because P is true" is using *circular reasoning*.

EXAMPLE A

There were once two little neighbor boys who wanted to eat a cookie together. But each of their mothers had said that they couldn't have any.

Sam: "I've got an idea. Why don't I take a cookie from my mother's jar, and we can share it. Then, Bill, you'll take a cookie from your mother's cookie jar and put it in my mother's jar."

Bill: "But then I will get in trouble 'cause my Mom will see a cookie gone."

Sam: "Then, we can take a cookie from my Mom's jar and put it in your Mom's jar, then she won't notice."

Sam: "No, then you will get in trouble."

Bill: "I don't get it. We're going in a circle here."

This is circular, and isn't getting these boys anywhere.

EXAMPLE B

Plaintiff: "Judge, I'm not lying here. I'm a religious person, and religious people don't lie."

Judge: "How do I know you are a religious person?"

Plaintiff: "Because I would never lie."

The plaintiff is using circular reasoning. The plaintiff is saying that he is a religious person, and since religious people don't lie, therefore he isn't lying. We have to assume that he isn't lying when he says he is a religious person! The plaintiff is going in circles, which is why this is called circular reasoning.

The plaintiff is essentially saying "P is true because Q is true, and Q is true because P is true," or "It's true because it's true." Circular arguments are *begging the question*. They assume the thing they are trying to prove. Some circular arguments can be very difficult to catch and unravel. They make you feel like you want to take your brain out and look at it.

PEANUTS reprinted by permission of United Feature Syndicate, Inc.

Circular reasoning. Girls are smarter because scientists have proven it. We know the scientists are right because they are girls, and girls are smarter.

EXAMPLE C

> Jimmy: "Dad, why do I have to learn logic?"
> Dad: "Because it will help to develop your mind."
> Jimmy: "Why will it develop my mind?"
> Dad: "Because it will help you think better."

Jimmy's Dad is using a very simple circular argument. He is simply repeating his first statement, but using different words to say the same thing. Johnny wants more proof, but his Dad won't give it. He did not actually answer his son's question. Sometimes when someone can't think of a better argument for something, then he simply restates his original argument in different words as proof for his old argument.

When someone tries to support an argument by just repeating his main premise, then he is using circular reasoning. If we said that "everyone should study logic because logic should be studied by everyone," we would be using circular reasoning.

EXAMPLE D

"To allow every man unbounded freedom of speech must always be, on the whole, advantageous to the state; for it is highly conducive to the interests of the community that each individual should enjoy a liberty, perfectly unlimited, of expressing his sentiments." – Richard Whately, in his book *Elements of Logic*, 1826.

This is a classic example of circular reasoning. Many famous and intelligent men have used circular reasoning like this without realizing it – and many others have used circular reasoning and did know that they were using it. Some naive people are so taken in by the magic of words that they never realize that an argument only went in a circle.

Exercises

A. Which of the following examples contain the fallacy of circular reasoning?

1. Person A: "Capital punishment for murder is perfectly justified."
   Person B: "Why is that?"
   Person A: "Because it is right for society to put to death those who have committed murder."

2. Politician running for Public Office: "You can all trust what I say. I have never lied in my life."

3. Woman: "It doesn't seem like you love me."
   Man: "Why is that?"
   Woman: "If you loved me, you would give me all your money."

4. "You shouldn't pray to the God of the Bible because he doesn't exist. But you should pray to your dead ancestors, because you couldn't pray to them if they didn't exist."

5. A: "I feel that astrology brings us closer to the truth about our future, don't you?"
   B: "No. I think it's stupid."
   A: "But I know it is true because I'm an Aries, and people born under the sign of Aries are very good at discovering the truth."

6. Teenager: "Who took my hair brush? I never can find it when I want it, and when I don't want it it's always right there."

7. Person who wants to study logic, but hasn't yet: "I know that all the people who want to study logic are very intelligent people. It's very simple. If they weren't so intelligent, then they wouldn't want to think logically! Obviously."

8. Husband: "I'm pooped. When we get home I'm going to sit and relax and eat in front of the TV. That's what I need to do."
   Wife: "And I suppose I'll have to work my fingers to the bone cooking that food you're going to eat…"
   Husband: "Why, who else would do it?"

9. News reporter after a debate: "My fellow Americans, these debates have given you the opportunity to observe a pessimistic candidate who nearsightedly hearkens us back to the defeatism and uncertainty of four years ago. You have also observed an inspiring, future-oriented optimist who believes in the strength and hope of America, and who wants to continue moving us forward. I am confident you will let your wisdom be clearly known at the polls."

10. Professor Sneedell: "All experienced experts in this field agree with my findings."
    Student: "But I heard that Professor Schilling disagrees with you."
    Professor Sneedell: "He isn't an experienced expert, so his views don't count."
    Student: "How do you know he doesn't have any experience in this field?"
    Professor Sneedell: "Obviously he must not have any experience, since he disagrees with me."

11. "We must accept the traditions of the men of old time who affirm themselves to be the offspring of the gods – that is what they say – and they must surely have known their own ancestors. How can we doubt the word of the children of the gods?" – Plato, *Timaeus*

B. What fallacy, if any, is committed in the following examples?

12. Advertisement: "Gary Cooper brushed his teeth with Colgate."

13. Yankee: "Yuck! You're eating grits! I don't see how you can stand them – they originated in the South, and southern foods taste terrible."

14. "Handgun Control Inc. says buying a gun will make you suicidal. I don't think I'll buy a gun. Those people at Handgun Control Inc. must be experts on guns."

C. Is there an example of circular reasoning in the following dialogue? If so, what is it?

15. Little Greek: "I think I have a cold."

Big German: "At least it isn't an echinacea cold."

Nosy Austrian: "What is an echinacea cold?"

Big German: "You take echinacea because you think you might be catching a cold, then when you stop taking it, you get an even worse cold because you've stopped."

Nosy Austrian: "What clinical studies have led you to believe this theory?"

Big German: "I know it's true because it happened to me."

Nosy Austrian: "But anecdotal evidence, especially just from one experience, isn't reliable."

Little Greek: "Real doctors don't recommend taking echinacea."

Nosy Austrian: "How do you know that? What are 'real' doctors?"

Little Greek: "Real doctors who go to college know more than those health-nut doctors like Dr. D—— who recommends taking herbs because he sells them."

Nosy Austrian: "How do you know the difference between a real doctor and the other kind?"

Little Greek: "Because real doctors are smarter."

Nosy Austrian: "How do you know that the IQ of doctors who do not recommend taking echinacea is higher than doctors who do recommend taking echinacea? Have you done studies on the different IQs of doctors?"

Little Greek: "It's obvious they are smarter. They don't recommend taking echinacea."

Nosy Austrian: "Our argument is going in a circle."

Little Greek: "No, it isn't."

Lesson 15

Equivocation

The fallacy of equivocation occurs when somebody walks up to you…

…and punches you in the nose. Now, this isn't normal behavior in civilized society, so you ask the offender about it: "Ow! Why'd you do that?"

He responds: "Today is Tuesday, and I can't stop myself from doing that on Tuesdays. I have a habit."

You, not satisfied by such a quizzical explanation, and hugging a hurting proboscis, say, "So, what does that have to do with anything?"

"Well," he says, "everybody is in the habit of doing something. You are probably in the habit of brushing your teeth in the morning. You're probably also in the habit of buckling your seat belt when you take a ride in a car. So, I see nothing wrong with my little habit."

Now, we all smell that there is something fishy going on with this story. Where is it coming from? The arguer is playing with his words. He is changing the meaning of the word "habit."

When he begins, "habit" means something someone does because he lacks self-control. He says: "I can't stop myself from doing that on Tuesdays. It's a habit." Habit, here, refers to things like biting your nails, cracking your knuckles or perpetually checking to see if your socks match. Later in the conversation, "habit" refers to something somebody is accustomed to doing often – but which is not bad. Getting up in the morning, eating breakfast, etc. are habits.

An *equivocation* changes the meaning of a word in the middle of an argument.

Sometimes the person who commits an equivocation isn't aware of it.

EXAMPLE B

"If the English don't drive on the right side of the road, what are they doing on the wrong side?"

Here, "right" changes meaning from right-hand versus left-hand, to right versus wrong.

EXAMPLE C

"We must indeed all hang together, or, most assuredly, we shall all hang separately." – Benjamin Franklin (at the signing of the Declaration of Independence.)

"Hang" changes meaning here from "keeps close company" to "being strung at the end of a rope." Equivocation is also used for humor.

EXAMPLE D

Dorothy: "Are you doing that on purpose, or can't you make up your mind?"
Scarecrow: "That's the trouble. I can't make up my mind. I haven't got a brain. Just straw."
Dorothy: "How can you talk if you haven't got a brain?"
Scarecrow: "I don't know. But some people without brains do an awful lot of talking, don't they?"
Dorothy: "Yes, I guess you're right."

The Scarecrow is changing the meaning of "brain." First, he is talking about someone who lacks a physical organ called a brain, and then he is talking about somebody who lacks wisdom or sense.

EXAMPLE E

"Everyone knows that laws change all the time. Prohibition was repealed after only a few years. Laws against criticizing the president were repealed. You see, the laws of thermodynamics, which say that it is impossible to make a true perpetual motion machine, can easily change, just like prohibition. My company is attempting to build a perpetual motion machine. I encourage you to invest in it."

This argument may sound convincing, until you look closely. The speaker first refers to law as a piece of legislation which is made by the government – such as the Constitution, or a speed limit ordinance. Then, he refers to law as a natural law, something which we see in nature which never changes – such as the laws of gravity and other scientific laws.

An equivocation. Hobbes' definition of "peck" is different than the math book's definition.

Exercises

A. What are the terms which have changed their meanings in these examples? How do the definitions differ?

1. Dad: "Go put the dogs in the pen." Son: "Aw, Dad, I couldn't do that. The dogs are too big. Besides, it would mess up all the ink, and the pen wouldn't write correctly."

2. Dad: "Son, when you grow up I want you always to be a responsible young man." Son: "But, Dad, I am already very responsible. Whenever something breaks around here, it seems like I am always responsible."

3. Communist Party speaker: "The Declaration of Independence says that 'all men are created equal.' But we see today anything but equality. The rich politician and businessman gorge themselves on luxuries, while poor people pick up trash out of the gutter. Nobody could say that is equal. Vote for the Communist Party and live up to the intentions of the Declaration of Independence."

4. "Apes, dolphins, and my dog Buster are all intelligent animals. They can all learn to do tricks and learn to have complicated social lives. I think it is wrong to say that man is the only intelligent being."

B. What fallacy, if any, is committed in the following examples?

5. A teenager: "I'm hungry. I wonder if there is something to eat in the refrigerator....Only leftover roast beef. I guess I'm not that hungry."

6. "Anybody who uses lots of fallacies has got to be very illogical. The book *The Fallacy Detective* uses lots of fallacies (as examples), so it must be a very illogical book."

7. "It is easy to prove that smoking causes cancer, because it has been shown conclusively that smoking is a carcinogenic agent."

8. "Achoo! I must have a cold ... maybe I had better put on a sweater."

9. Clyde: "Good grief, I've been working every day for two weeks straight.
   Bert: "Why don't you tell your boss that you want a raise because you work so hard?"
   Clyde: "I can't get in touch with him. He's on vacation."

10. "Half this game is ninety percent mental." – Yogi Berra

11. Computer: "This program has performed an illegal operation and will be terminated."
    Jenny: "Ahhhh! I'm a criminal! Are they going to throw me in prison?"

12. Young parent: "My uncle says you shouldn't spank kids when they are bad. He says it stunts their growth. My uncle must be right; he works as an engineer and he is pretty smart."

13. Advertisement: "This university is the best place to go to school. After all, there is no better place than U of DB to find great friends, learn to improve yourself, and accomplish all those great things you are capable of doing."

14. "Who did you pass on the road?" the King went on, holding out his hand to the Messenger for some hay.
"Nobody," said the Messenger.
"Quite right," said the King. "This lady saw him too. So of course Nobody walks slower than you."
"I do my best," the Messenger said in a sullen tone. "I'm sure nobody walks much faster than I do!"
"He can't do that," said the King, "or else he'd have been here first!"
– *Through the Looking-Glass* by Lewis Carroll

15. "That place is so crowded that nobody goes there anymore." – Yogi Berra

16. "I hate Friday the 13th. That day is unlucky. My uncle fell off of a tightrope last Friday the 13th."

Lesson 16

Loaded Question

When someone asks two questions, but one is hidden behind the other, that's a *loaded question*.

EXAMPLE A

"Gimme dat." Four-year-old Bridget grabs a toy shovel from her brother Sam. "Oughhhhhh!" Sam grabs after the fleet form of Bridget. "Give me back my shovel...!" He trips, sprawling on the sandy beach. Scurrying like a crab, she giggles, "I want it." Running after her, Sam throws a handful of sand at Bridget, still out of reach. Bridget stops and hurls the shovel in Sam's direction, wailing, "Mawwww, Sam took my shovel and got sand in my eyes. Waaaaahh-hhhaaahh."

Looking up, Mother asks sharply, "Sam, come here. Why did you take that shovel from your baby sister?"

Mother has asked a loaded question. Her question contained two questions rolled into one. She should have first asked, "Sam, did you take that shovel from Bridget?" before she asked, "Why did you take that shovel from Bridget?" Sam may not have actually taken the shovel from Bridget.

EXAMPLE B

Judge: "Prosecution, you may now cross-examine the witness."

Prosecutor: "Mr. Blanchard, what did you use to wipe your fingerprints off this gun?"

Defendant, Mr. Blanchard: "I didn't use anything."

Prosecutor: "You left your fingerprints on the gun, then?"

Mr. Blanchard: "No! I've never seen that gun."

Prosecutor: "But you just said you never wiped your fingerprints off this gun."

Defense Attorney: "Your Honor, the Prosecution is trying to confuse my client…"

Prosecutor: "Okay. Let me ask a different question. Mr. Blanchard, have you stopped beating your wife?"

Mr. Blanchard: "No."

Prosecutor: "Then, have you ever felt so guilty for being so abusive to your wife?"

Mr. Blanchard: "I never abused my wife."

Prosecutor: "But you just said you haven't stopped beating her. Any intelligent person on the jury knows that if you still beat your wife, then you are an abusive husband."

Mr. Blanchard: "I never said I beat my wife! You asked…"

The prosecution is trying to confuse the defendant by asking loaded questions. These questions contain hidden assumptions, and Mr. Blanchard is having trouble understanding how to answer them. If he answers "yes" to the question, "Have you stopped beating your wife," then everybody in the court will think that Mr. Blanchard used to beat his wife. If he answers "no," then everyone will think that he still beats his wife.

The purpose of a loaded question is to make you assume the answer to a hidden question, without actually asking that hidden question.

EXAMPLE C

Question from a *Wall Street Journal*/NBC News poll: "Do you favor sending ground troops if it is the only way to stop the fighting in Bosnia?"

The respondents to this poll unwittingly answered more than one question. This poll question is an example of a loaded question. No matter how you answer the question, your true feelings on the matter may not be voiced. The two questions should be "Do you think we should try to stop the fighting?" and, "Would you favor sending in ground troops to stop it?" In other words, the poll assumed that all respondents believe that it is the United State's business to stop the fighting in Bosnia. The poll should not have assumed this.

Many Americans did not think that the United States should be involved in the war in Bosnia, but the views of these Americans never appeared in the results of this poll.

When you suspect that someone is asking you a loaded question, then ask yourself how you can split the question. Before answering the question, you need to question the question – be aware of the assumptions behind it. Then you can more accurately answer what they are asking.

Exercises

A. Which of the following arguments contain a loaded question? If an argument contains a loaded question, explain what the unstated question is.

1. Neighbor: "Why do you like to disturb the neighborhood by playing your music so loud everybody can hear it a mile away?"

2. Advertisement: "So, when are you going to make the new Ford Bubblebox your first car?"

3. Mother to child: "When was the last time you took a bath?"

4. Letter to the editor: "I am just furious about the Mayor's handling of this new city ordinance designed to protect environmentally sensitive residents. What is he going to do when the state tourism bureau lists us as the worst-smelling city just because thoughtless people are allowed to burn their leaves and make everybody else suffer? The question I'd like to ask the Mayor is: what is he going to do when we civic-minded residents protest his actions and start burning our leaves in front of city hall? What's that going to do for his city beautification project?"

5. Magazine ad: "Does the pain medication you use now start to work in less than one second?"

6. Commercial for security system: "Can your business run the risk of computer hackers breaking into your most sensitive files?"

7. Child to mother: "Why did God make bathtubs? So he could torture little children by making their mother give them a bath?"

8. Phone salesman: "Yes, madam, our company sells only the best kitchen utensils…. Yes, we guarantee everything we sell for three days or your money back…. Certainly, we never pressure you to buy more products down the road. What will it be, check, cash, or credit card? I can take any form of payment that is convenient for you…."

9. Person A: "You think too much."
Person B: "No, I'm just not good at making quick decisions."

B. What fallacy, if any, is committed in the following examples?

10. "The Cubs must be a good baseball team. They are very popular in their hometown of Chicago."

11. "Not everyone can be famous, because some of us have to be less popular than everybody else."

12. Mom: "Do you know where my *Reader's Digest* is?"
Jenny: "It might have been eaten by the dog."

13. "It is commonly known that, of all the living creatures on this planet, man is the only rational being. Therefore, we can conclude that women are irrational."

14. "Every time I go to the store, I end up buying something I don't need and forgetting everything I came for."

Lesson 17

Part-to-Whole

When someone tries to say that what is true of part of something must also be true of the whole thing together, then this person is using the *part-to-whole fallacy*. (In the next lesson you will learn the whole-to-part fallacy, which is very similar.)

EXAMPLE A

Child: "Mommy, why is this feather pillow so heavy? It's just got feathers in it, and little feathers don't weigh anything."

Sometimes it is hard for little children to understand that even though a part of something weighs very little, the whole thing altogether may weigh much more. A million little blades of grass added together in a bale of hay can weigh a ton or more.

EXAMPLE B

Jenny: "You won't believe how good this wedding cake is going to be. I'm only using the best ingredients. It has 17 pounds of imported Dutch chocolate, 256 candied maraschino cherries, 65 organic farm-fresh duck eggs…"

Jenny is assuming that the quality of the ingredients in her cake will guarantee the quality of the finished product – but she may never have baked a cake in her life! The quality of the cake may turn out to be very different from the quality of the ingredients.

EXAMPLE C

Bart: "What on earth are you doing? You look like you are building the Statue of Liberty out of paper clips!"

Ben: "You guessed it. I've just started. All I have is the structure outlined."

Bart: "That's a brainless idea – it'll look stupid. Anybody knows you can't make something beautiful out of ugly old paper clips."

Bart thinks that because paper clips are commonplace, therefore anything made from paper clips must also be commonplace. This is the part-to-whole fallacy, where someone thinks that the character of the parts is the character of the whole thing altogether.

EXAMPLE D

Hans: "We know our logic book doesn't have flaws in it because we checked every page and each one is flawless, and therefore this is a flawless logic book."

Nathaniel: "If any of our readers find a mistake in our book, then the printer must have done it."

We know this is true because we logicians are experts at detecting mistakes, and so any book written by a logician can't be mistaken.

Actually that last sentence was also a part-to-whole fallacy. Just because every page in this logic book has no mistakes does not prove that there are not larger mistakes throughout the whole book – for instance a mistake in the order of the lessons, or a mistake in the ideas we teach. But we've decided to blame the printer if we find any.

Exercises

A. Which of the following arguments contain a *part-to-whole fallacy*?

1. Johnny: "If logicians are experts at organized thinking, does that mean that a convention of logicians would be well organized?"

2. "Team America was selected from all the best players in the United States. Since they are all the best at their positions, this team is going to win."

3. "I know that rich people pay more taxes. They give almost 50% of what they make to the government. It's obvious that the rich contribute more money towards the running of our nation than the middle classes."

4. Writer: "I know why I have writer's block today. It's cloudy outside and that makes me feel depressed and uncreative." Critic: "Don't let yourself think that way. You'll always be able to think of some excuse for why you don't have to make yourself accomplish something." Writer: "Then maybe it's because I started the first part of my day with too big of a breakfast. That can make me feel tired for the whole morning."

5. "...the universe is spherical in form...because all the constituent parts of the universe, that is the sun, moon, and the planets appear in this form." – Nicolaus Copernicus, *The New Idea of the Universe*

6. "Seeing that the eye and hand and foot and every one of our members has some obvious function, must we not believe that in like manner a human being has a function over and above those particular functions?" – Aristotle, in *Nicomachean Ethics*

7. Royal Joker: "No one laughs at my jokes anymore. It must be because I don't have enough little bells on my hat."

8. Rich husband to his wife: "Dear, I haven't spared a penny to get the most exquisite materials and furnishings for our new home. I hope you're happy. It's the best house money could buy." Wife: "Why does this marble floor in the dining room seem to slope down towards the kitchen? Look! The zebra wood dining table is sliding towards the dumbwaiter! And what are the bronze electrical outlets doing in the vaulted ceiling? How am I supposed to reach them? And why does the hall light switch make all the toilets flush? And why does steaming water spout out of the drain into my face when I turn on the faucet? And what is a smoke detector doing inside the fireplace?"

9. Advertisement: "The suits here at Le Bouboudetteux are tailored to the highest standards. We offer our customers distinction and class.

10. Farmer: "Look at that field of corn. The whole thing looks so perfectly beautiful!"

11. Johnny: "Dad, this logic book by the Bluedorn boys has a mistake in it. It says 'whole-to-part' here, and it should say 'part-to-whole.' If the Bluedorn boys are logicians, and they don't know how to tell their logical fallacies apart, then I don't think I should be studying logic at all – the whole subject of logic is probably one big mix-up."

B. What fallacy, if any, is committed in the following examples?

12. "It would be a crime to pass up another helping of this lasagne. I don't want to go to jail, so I had better have a little more."

13. "What other explanation can there be for all the evidence supporting mental telepathy, than the explanation that mental telepathy is humankind's way of interfacing with the spirit world?"

14. "We all have the obligation to help those who are less fortunate. Not every person can be expected to be rich, and therefore some people need the aid of those with better resources."

15. Prosecuting Attorney: "What were you doing on the night of the murder?"
    Witness: "Say, did anybody ever tell you that you have a striking resemblance to Gary Cooper?"

16. "This book on psychology says childrearing should not be done by the parents of the child. It should be done by the government. It says parents harm their children when they try to teach them. What an interesting idea. I didn't know I was hurting my poor little Johnny."

Lesson 18

Whole-to-Part

When someone tries to say that what is true of something as a whole must also be true of each of its parts, then this person is using the *whole-to-part fallacy*. This fallacy is the reverse of the *part-to-whole fallacy*. It's easy to get these two fallacies mixed up – they are so similar.

EXAMPLE A

Part-to-whole:
Little Wilber at the beginning of the family picnic: "If I can pull apart one earthworm with my fingers, Mommy, why can't I pull apart a handful of earthworms?"

Whole-to-part:
Little Wilber at the end of the family picnic: "If our bag of potato chips won't float when I throw it in the pond, why will one of my potato chips float by itself?"

Little Wilber doesn't understand that individual earthworms and individual potato chips have different qualities by themselves than when they are in large groups.

EXAMPLE B

Part-to-whole:
Anarchist college student: "What's wrong with killing people? We humans are just made of all the food we ate last year – digested and made into skin and bones. If I shoot you, I'm just rearranging a bunch of former hamburgers and French fries."

Whole-to-part:

Health-conscious college student: "The bristlecone pine trees are said to live for thousands of years. That's why I take a capsule each day of dried bristlecone pine bark. I think it will help me live longer."

The anarchist college student believed that humans are nothing more than what we eat. But the Bible says that humans are more than just the atoms and molecules which make up our bodies. And the health-conscious student thought that the long-living qualities of the bristlecone pines could be captured by eating little bits of the pine tree bark. But whatever causes the bristlecone pines to live a long time may be a quality which is only in the tree as a whole, not in each little piece of bark.

DILBERT reprinted by permission of United Feature Syndicate, Inc.

Whole-to-part fallacy. Just because scientists may be generally smarter,
this does not mean that each individual scientist is smart.

One way to tell the difference between a part-to-whole and a whole-to-part fallacy is to look at the conclusion of the argument. A conclusion which says something about the *whole* is a part-to-whole fallacy. A conclusion which says something about just *part* of the whole is a whole-to-part fallacy.

We must understand that the whole is often more than just the parts, and the parts don't always have the qualities of the whole. If we don't make this distinction, then we may commit the part-to-whole fallacy, or the whole-to-part fallacy.

Exercises

A. Which of the following examples contain a part-to-whole fallacy, a whole-to-part fallacy, or neither?

1. Inept guy trying to fix his car in his backyard: "My car is a General Motors car, so every part must be made by GM."

2. Shopkeeper: "The Smith family has always been hardworking and creative; I don't doubt that Bubba Smith will make a good employee."

3. Farmer: "I know from experience that this farm can produce about 200 bushels of corn per acre. I think this area on the side of this hill will be a fertile place to plant our garden."

4. Conservative politician: "If each individual person is the best at managing his own interests, than won't society become the most efficient when we maximize individual liberty?"

5. Businessman: "I don't think I can go wrong to invest in the Pffizt-Hickup Amalgamated Tweezers Factory. Everybody knows the whole economy is booming."

6. Woodsman hunting for his lost ax: "If I keep searching in this part of the forest, I might never find what I'm looking for."

7. Newspaper columnist: "If each American resolves to be more aware of the dangers around us, then we as a society will be able to feel safer in our daily lives."

8. News report: "Over the past hundred years, the residents of Ikabiki have torn down the royal palace and have taken little parts of it to their homes. They do this in the hope that they can make their homes more elegant with the timbers, hunks of stone, and pieces of iron stair-railing which once made up the most magnificent architectural accomplishment of the Ikabiki civilization."

9. Sports reporter: "In this year's games, Team America has won more medals than any other team in history. So Jim, who's on the Team America, must be a great athlete."

10. President of Stohl-and-DeLeigh, Attorneys at Law: "Harvard Law School is a very prestigious school. I'm sure this new lawyer must be well trained, since he graduated from Harvard."

11. A desperate little ax, looking for the woodsman who lost it in the woods: "If I just poke part of my handle up a little higher, my master might see me. Oh! He's looking this way!"

12. Exuberant college student: "The Reformation in Europe in the 1500s and 1600s was a grand movement from God to bring His people back to the truth. That's why I've decided to become a Presbyterian, since Presbyterians are Reformed."

B. What fallacy, if any, is committed in the following examples?

13. Farmer to his family: "Which one of you left the pasture gate open and let all the cows out?"

14. Man: "It is well known that men are more intelligent than women since their heads are bigger and thus their brain size is larger. Clearly, then, brain size is correlated with intelligence, since the evidence shows that people with larger brains are also more intelligent."

15. "Those are my reasons for doing it, but, since you never listen to reason, you'll ignore them."

16. "Everybody's going to see the new movie *The Day of the Spatulas*. It has been the most popular movie for weeks. It must be a movie with a good plot, strong characters, and strong moral values."

17. "The First Lady thinks everyone should learn to read, and learn to read well. It must be very important."

Lesson 19

Either-Or

When someone asserts that we must choose between two things, when in fact we have more than two alternatives, he is using the *either-or fallacy.*

EXAMPLE A

Patrick Henry: "Give me liberty or give me death!"

News Reporter: "Don't you think that's a bit extreme?"

Henry: "What? That I would be willing to lay down my life for my country?"

Reporter: "No. It's just you're shouting in my ear."

Henry: "Your forefathers sacrificed their lives, their fortunes and their sacred honor in order to pass their freedoms on to their children – freedoms which you now enjoy! And you ask me to lower my voice! Have you no shame?"

Reporter: "Well, maybe you have a point there, but what about your ultimatum? Aren't there any other options?"

Henry: "Options! We colonists are about to be shackled hand and foot by that foul tyrant King George, and you want me to give you options! I tell you that no choice remains for us today but the choice between fighting for liberty, and death as slaves!"

Reporter: "Hey, man, like I can think of a few more options. What about moving to Tahiti?"

Henry: "Give me liberty or give me Tahiti.... Somehow I don't think that one will go over well with General Washington."

Obviously Patrick Henry's original argument was much different from this one. But *taken only by itself,* Henry's statement "Give me liberty or give me death!" sets up a false dilemma between two choices.

When someone tries to use this fallacy, usually one of the options is so absurd that we are forced to choose the other option. This fallacy becomes obvious once we realize that there are often more than two choices.

EXAMPLE B

> Johnny: "Either you study logic with me, Dad, or else I won't do it."
> Dad: "What's this again?"

Johnny really isn't trying to prove anything to his Dad; he just doesn't want to do another school subject. So, Johnny has set up a false dilemma. But his Dad solves it by offering a third alternative:

> Dad: "There's another option; you either study logic, or you're grounded for a month. That just about exhausts the alternatives."

EXAMPLE C

> Mother-in-law: "Maria, dear, you aren't going to send Johnny to the public school to grow up as a brainwashed couch potato, are you!"
> Daughter-in-law: "No."
> Mother-in-law: "Good. Then let's not say anything else bad about Miss Cecilia's Institute. I'll just ignore your comments about my son's experiences with those dear teachers. I'm sure he doesn't remember it correctly. He wasn't always the most perfect little boy, you know."
> Daughter-in-law: "Jim said they eat little…"
> Mother-in-law: "Now don't give me anymore of that. Three generations of DeMedichis have received only the best education at Miss Cecilia's. We're not going to change that, are we! Now, that's settled."
> Daughter-in-law: "We're not sending him there."
> Mother-in-law: "But if we all agree that the public school is not a place for someone in our family, then the teachers at Miss Cecilia's are our only option in this city. You aren't going to move away from our beautiful city are you?"
> Daughter-in-law: "No. We're going to homeschool him."
> Mother-in-law: "You are going to do what! Oh, I feel one of my spells coming on! Where are my smelling salts! Maria, help me to the couch…."

When a person is strongly committed to a particular viewpoint he often ignores or suppresses possible alternatives.

EXAMPLE D

Doctor to a distraught woman: "I'm afraid your husband will either survive the operation, or not. There are no other options."

In this case, when there are truly only two possibilities, then an "either-or" form of argument is not a fallacy.

Exercises

A. Choose which of the following arguments use either-or reasoning, and which do not.

1. Corn farmer to another corn farmer: "Nobody can make a living growing corn. Either the rain is good and we have lots of corn, but the price is low and we lose money; or else there is a drought, and we don't have any corn to sell, even though the price is high."

2. Mafia thugs to their captive: "Either yer fer us or yer agin' us. And it don't look like yer fer us. So, we're gonna make sure you don' interfere. Come 'ere Tony…"

3. There is a story that Socrates' wife, when she heard that he was condemned to death, said: "Those wretched judges have condemned him to death unjustly!" And Socrates replied: "Would you really prefer that I were justly condemned?"

4. The bandit shouts into the upturned stagecoach: "Throw out yer va-u-bls' m'ladies, or I'a shoot!"

5. Mother to child: "Either you take a bath now, or you take a bath after you are done making those mud pies."

6. Neuropsychologist: "A genius is either born a genius or his environment makes him that way. A little familiarity with the lives of many of the world's geniuses shows that their environment was not always a good influence. If environment isn't an important factor, we can come to only one conclusion: geniuses are born geniuses."

7. Coach to his team: "Nice guys finish last."

8. Gardener to his apprentice: "If you don't water these plants, they'll die!"

9. Father to hungry children: "We're not millionaires around here. Would you like rice with bugs in it, biscuit with weevils in it, or to go to bed hungry again?"

10. Grumpy old lady: "It must have been raining, snowing, sleeting, or hailing earlier, because the streets are wet. It couldn't be snow or sleet because it's July. It couldn't be hail because I haven't heard any thunderstorms. So it must have rained."

11. Hysterical mother to her husband: "You've got to teach the boys logic! If you don't teach them logic, they won't learn how to think! And they'll become atheists and die in prison! Don't you care about your sons?"

B. What fallacy, if any, is committed in the following examples?

12. "As the nation approaches a new millennium, what are the most important priorities facing our next president? (1) Saving Social Security, strengthening Medicare, and paying on the debt, (2) or implementing (Texas Gov.) George W. Bush's $1.7 trillion risky tax scheme that overwhelmingly benefits the wealthy?" – Questions from a weekly Internet poll on the Democratic National Committee web site.

13. "I know why I have been in a bad mood for so long. It's because my frame of mind hasn't been good."

14. "Over the years, technology has progressed so that today science can do miracles. We have automobiles, computers, and individually wrapped cheese slices. Yet, look at the miracles in the Bible. The same people who praise modern scientific miracles say the miracles in the Bible are impossible. This is a contradiction."

15. "Picasso's paintings must look very beautiful. They are very popular."

16. "Abortion is wrong. It says so right here in this book on contemporary home design."

17. College Professor: "As an individual, I believe it is good for me to plan and control all the decisions in my life. And that's why I believe, as a society, we should let the government control all aspects of our society."

18. Father, before sitting down to dinner: "Now, I want to know who took the fingernail clippers and hid them under the couch?"

19. Government official in a third-world country: "We should be able to trust this new American economic consultant. He's an American, and America is the land of free enterprise. He can't be a socialist."

C. 20. Which is correct to say:
   a. "The milk the cows *is* drinking is white," or,
   b. "The milk the cows *are* drinking is white"?

5

Statistical Fallacies

Lesson 20

What Is a Generalization?

We all generalize about things. That is, we all make broad comments about a group of people or kind of things.

EXAMPLE A

"No matter what they say, all salesmen don't care a bit about the people they sell to. They just want your money."

We say this because we have met many salesmen, heard from our friends about many salesmen, or been salesmen once ourselves. We don't say this because we have known every salesman personally. We generalize every day, and this is often useful. (See, that last sentence was a generalization.)

We make predictions about what somebody is going to do before he does it, and sometimes we are right.

EXAMPLE B

You are playing a game of Clue with Jenny and Bert. Bert, after one of his turns, lays down his cards with a crooked smile and begins to study the ceiling unconcernedly. You have seen that look before. That means he has the solution, and he is about to win the game. Next turn, he wins.

You knew he would win because you generalized. You noticed that he did those things in past games when he won, and you generalized that he would do the same every time he won at Clue.

Elements of a Generalization

A generalization is composed of samples taken from a class.

A *class* is a group of people or things which all have some common characteristic or characteristics.

(1) All salesmen, (2) all used car salesmen, (3) all jelly beans, (4) all times Bert wins Clue. These are all classes of people or things.

When you examine one or more of the people or things in a class, then you are taking a *sample* of that class.

We examine: (1) one salesman, (2) two used car salesmen, (3) all the jelybeans in this dish, (4) the last four times Bert won Clue.
All these are samples of their individual classes.

A *generalization* is taking a sample from a class of things, then, using the information from that sample, saying something about everything in that class.

If we generalized from the above examples, we might come up with something such as: (1) all salesmen are rich, (2) most used car salesmen are money grubbers, (3) 22.099% of jelly beans in the world are black, (4) every time Bert wins Clue, he looks up at the ceiling in that way.
Unless we know what we are doing, taking samples and making generalizations can be a risky business. When our samples and generalizations are not conducted properly, they are called "hasty generalizations."
We will discuss hasty generalizations more below.

A Few Comments on Generalizations

I. THERE IS NOTHING ABSOLUTELY CERTAIN ABOUT GENERALIZATIONS

— A GENERALIZATION IS EITHER STRONG OR WEAK.

Generalizations are useful because we don't need to study every single item within a class before we draw a conclusion about the entire class.

EXAMPLE C

For this year's research project, Bert wants to find out how many politicians in the world are corrupt. Since it is very tedious to examine every politician on the planet to check which ones ever took a bribe, Bert is going to take a sample of 3,000,000 politicians from all over the world, then generalize from that sample. He finds that every single politician he surveyed took at least one bribe and was therefore corrupt. He concludes that all politicians are corrupt.

Bert is probably satisfied with his results. However, Bert never *really* knows whether his generalization is correct until he examines every single politician. There is always the chance that later he will find a politician who isn't corrupt. Then he would have to change his generalization: "Not *all* politicians are corrupt."

Therefore, a generalization cannot be true or false; it can be only strong or weak. A strong generalization is one which is more likely to be correct.

2. A GENERALIZATION RELIES UPON SAMPLES OF A CLASS. IT DOES NOT RELY UPON A STUDY OF EVERY SINGLE MEMBER OF THE CLASS.

If Bert examined every single politician (the class here is "all politicians"), and found that every one was corrupt, he wouldn't be generalizing when he said, "All politicians are corrupt." He would be stating what he knew to be true.

3. ANY GENERALIZATION MUST BE EITHER ADJUSTED OR OVERTHROWN BY A SINGLE CONTRARY CASE.

If Bert studied 3,000,000 politicians all over the world, and found that they were all corrupt, he might generalize that all politicians are corrupt. But, if he later finds a single politician who isn't corrupt (maybe he is living off in the jungle somewhere and didn't show up for the census) he would have to at least modify his generalization: "All politicians are corrupt – *except one* whom I know of." Or better, "*Almost* all politicians are corrupt."

4. A GENERALIZATION BECOMES STRONGER AS THE SAMPLE GROWS LARGER AND MORE REPRESENTATIVE.

A good generalization examines a large sample which reaches to all corners of the class being studied. We'll study this more a little later.

Exercises

A. Decide whether the following exercises are generalizations. Assume the speaker is telling the truth about his findings.

1. "I talked to my boss last Monday and he yelled at me.
Josie talked to the boss right after Memorial Day and he yelled at her.
Reginald talked to the boss yesterday evening and he yelled at him.
Conclusion: the boss always yells at people who try to talk to him."

2. "All German Shepherd dogs are ferocious. I have owned four German Shepherd dogs and they were all ferocious."

3. "Every single German Shepherd I have ever seen was kindhearted and gentle. I think the German Shepherd breed is kindhearted and gentle."

4. "All dogs have fleas. I just finished examining every single dog in the universe, and they all have fleas."

5. "People are living longer, happier lives. Over 767 seniors were asked questions about their health, well-being, financial situation, and general happiness. The study found that about 86% of seniors claimed that they felt as if they were living lives which were longer and happier than their parents'. Ethel Murdock, 76, of Palm Park Florida, said: 'My parents lived very hard lives on the farm, even when they were older, but I have it easy now.' "

6. "There are parts of Alaska which have a high elevation. Mount McKinley is 20,320 feet high."

7. Premise One: All novels by Charles Dickens are boring.
   Premise Two: *Great Expectations* is a novel by Charles Dickens.
   Conclusion: *Great Expectations* is boring.

8. "Studies have shown that women, on average, earn less than men do."

9. "The best way to catch any thief is to think like one."

10. Person A: "I think Mr. Washington is going to be the winner of the presidential election."
    Person B: "Why?"
    Person A: "Because I can't think of a single person who is going to vote for someone else, and I have talked with a lot of people."

11. Person A: "Mr. Washington is going to win the election."
    Person B: "Why do you think that. Have you been talking to some more of your friends?"
    Person A: "No. I just remembered – Mr. Washington is the only person running for office."

12. Farmer McDonald: "Farmers in the country can't make a dime at farming these days. I haven't made a penny this year."
    Farmer Brown: "That's not true. *The Farmer's Journal* asked four hundred farmers in California, and almost all of them said they made plenty of money this year."

13. "If I remember right, the last time the Cubs won the World Series was around 1910. The Cubs haven't won a World Series in almost a century."

14. "I want to take a trip out west. I think it would be fun. Last year we went to Colorado, and we had a lot of fun."

B. BONUS: Find an example of a generalization in the newspaper or television news.

Lesson 21

Hasty Generalizations

The most common logical fallacy is the hasty generalization. Ah, there we go with another generalization.

A *hasty generalization* is generalizing about a class based upon a small or poor sample.

When we buy things, we tend to make generalizations about brands. Out here in the wilds of Illinois, farmers own at least one pickup truck to drive – the major pickup – and several "backup" pickups which serve as lawn ornaments.

Every farmer bears allegiance to one brand of pickup over another. Certain farmers are Ford farmers, and others are Chevy farmers. (A growing minority are Dodge farmers.) Each thinks his brand is the best.

And the reason for their allegiance? "Well," Farmer McDonald will say, "I once owned a Ford, and it was junk. Now I only drive Chevies."

All of Farmer McDonald's experience with Ford trucks have come from this single sample. Is that a good sample from which to judge all Ford trucks? When pressed further, Farmer McDonald will confess that his unfortunate Ford really was junk, 15-year-old junk, bought used, and all Farmer McDonald's subsequent Chevies have been bought new and sold early. So his sample of Ford trucks may not be representative.

Down the road, Farmer Brown has a similar story: "I only buy Ford trucks. I once owned a Chevy and it was junk." Of course, farmer Brown's dilapidated Chevy had also seen better days before he nursed it home for the first time.

Maybe Ford trucks are junk. Maybe Chevy trucks are junk. But while Farmer McDonald and Farmer Brown may be right to call their own trucks "junk," they need to see many more trucks before they can accurately say all of the opposition's trucks are junk. Their generalizations are hasty.

Some Ways in Which People Make Hasty Generalizations

1. TOO SMALL OF A SAMPLE

Hasty generalizations commonly do not take a large enough sample. If our sample is not large enough, then we risk it not being representative of the class we are studying.

We all know that statistics indicate that tossing a coin will result in it landing half the time heads, and half the time tails. However, this does not mean that if we toss it four times we will see heads twice and tails twice. Even if we toss it a dozen times, we might not see an equal number of heads and tails. In order to actually see the heads and tails even out, we need to toss it many, many more times – say, a hundred or a thousand or more – yet even then we may be off by a few.

Obviously, Farmer McDonald and Farmer Brown did not take large enough samples for their generalizations. The trucks they bought may simply have been the duds which come out of any factory, or they may have been worn-out secondhand vehicles.

2. NOT A REPRESENTATIVE SAMPLE

Sometimes the sample for a generalization is large, but it isn't representative of the entire class.

If we wanted to know the eating habits of Italians, it would be very easy for us to study the Italians who live in our town. However, there are many Italians in the world: those who live in America and have or have not adhered to their regional fare; those who still live in Italy; those who are or aren't in the Mafia; those who are on a diet....

The Italians in our town may not eat the same things as those who live somewhere else. This study could conclude that most Italians eat only spaghetti, when in reality, just those in our town eat only spaghetti. Perhaps

Italians everywhere else eat pizza and ravioli. Perhaps we only studied Italians when they ate supper and found that they ate spaghetti then – but the rest of the time they ate Pop-Tarts.

Farmer McDonald and Farmer Brown's trucks also weren't representative of the "average" truck of their kind. There are many kinds of trucks in various states of decay. Their trucks were old and broken down. They would need to see a few examples which were not.

Exercises

A. In the following exercises, answer these questions: (a) Is it a generalization? (b) If so, how large is the sample which is being taken? (c) In your opinion, is the generalization strong or hasty? Why? Assume the speaker is telling the truth about his findings.

1. "All plumbers are brilliant. I know a plumber who can calculate the value of pi to the 289,954th digit."

2. "All plumbers are rich. I just went to the international plumbers convention and studied 3,000 plumbers there. They all made over $100,000 a year."

3. "My mom teaches people well. Whenever she explains something to me, I understand it perfectly."

4. "Some plumbers are brilliant. I'm a plumber, and I know I'm brilliant."

5. "Everything written by Charles Dickens is boring to me. I have read all his novels, and they all put me to sleep."

6. "Mr. Carl took some aspirin for a headache. A few minutes later he had an upset stomach. The next two times he had a headache, he did the same thing, with the same results. He then decided to not take aspirin for headaches. Instead, he took some other pain reliever, and he did not get an upset stomach. Mr. Carl then started taking aspirin again, and found that every time he took it, he had an upset stomach. Mr. Carl concluded that any time he takes aspirin, he will get an upset stomach."

7. "A barrel contains 100,000 jelly beans. After mixing up the barrel thoroughly (taking care that no jelly beans were squashed), we extract 5,000 jelly beans. 500 jelly beans are black. Therefore, 10% of the jelly beans in the barrel are black."

8. "A satellite survey of all of Colorado determined that the average elevation of the state was 6,806 feet."

9. "Southerners talk fast. I was just on the phone with one and he sure talked fast."

B. Evaluate these conclusions. Based upon your own knowledge of the subject, decide whether the conclusion is probably true or probably false. If you don't know enough about the subject to decide, then determine what you would need to know before you could draw a conclusion.

Example conclusion: Most McDonald's hamburgers are squashed by the time we get them.

Example answer: I think this is probably true. I have been to McDonald's restaurants all over the country and they always serve squashed hamburgers. Or (if you don't know much about the subject), I would need to eat hamburgers at many McDonald's restaurants rest all over the world before I could decide whether this is true.

10. "Most revolutions are bloody."

11. "Mrs. X (pick someone you know) seems to always act happy."

12. "Pigs are dirty animals."

13. "Hairstylists tend to be talkative."

14. "Firstborn children are always willful and tend to be spoiled."

15. "I am a below-average typist."

16. "Americans make more money than citizens of other countries."

17. "Almost all the people who live south of the Mason-Dixon Line speak with a drawl."

18. "The more people there are on welfare, the worse the economy becomes."

19. "Communist governments end in failure."

C. BONUS: Find an example of a hasty generalization in the newspaper or the evening news. Look for broad statements ("all," "always," "most," "many") and see how well these statements are supported.

Lesson 22

What Is an Analogy?

We are reasoning by *analogy* when we compare two items with each other.

EXAMPLE A

Bert: "My dad just bought a new car – it's a Ford."

Clyde: "Oh, really? My dad just bought a new Ford a few months ago. What size engine does yours have?"

Bert: "V-8."

Clyde: "Ours has a V-8 too. What color is it?"

Bert: "Blue."

Clyde: "So is ours. Boy, our cars are a lot alike. Ours drives very fast. I wonder if yours does?"

Bert: "I don't know yet, but if both our cars are so much alike, our new car must be fast too."

Bert is reasoning by analogy.

We are *reasoning by analogy* when we compare two or more items with each other. We notice that these items are the same in one or more respects, and conclude that they will be the same in other ways also.

Many useful observations can be gained through reasoning by analogy – if it is done properly.

EXAMPLE B

Mr. Smith: "The last time we went to the Joneses' for dinner, we ate salmon, and we were sick for the rest of the evening. The time before that, when we went to the Joneses', we ate salmon, and we were sick for the whole evening. Now, the Joneses have invited us over again and they are serving salmon – I'll bet we get sick."

In this analogy Mr. Smith is comparing the last two times they visited the Joneses with this time.

First evening: visit Joneses … Ate salmon … Got sick.
Second evening: visit Joneses … Ate salmon … Got sick
This evening: will visit Joneses … Will eat salmon … _____

Mr. Smith sees a pattern, and fills in the blank with "will get sick."

Analogies – like generalizations – are either strong or weak. As with a generalization, we never *really* know whether our analogy is correct until we actually examine the item in question. We don't *know* if Bert's dad's car is fast until we drive it. We don't *know* if Mr. Smith is going to get sick until that evening is over. Therefore, we can't say an analogy is true or false. We can only say an analogy is strong or weak. A strong analogy is one which is likely to be true.

When examining an analogy, we must not only think of areas where the two items are the same. We must also think of areas where the two items are different. How is Bert's parents' car different from Clyde's parents' car? Maybe Bert's is a large pickup truck and Clyde's is a small sports car. These differences can easily change the strength of an analogy. Two items can have a lot in common, and also have a lot not in common.

Poetic Analogies

While in this chapter we are mostly dealing with scientific analogies – the kind people use to prove things – there are other types of analogies.

Analogy is also used by authors to make a point.

EXAMPLE C

"The difference between the right word and the almost right word is the difference between lightning and the lightning bug." – Mark Twain

Here, Mark Twain compares the difference between "the right word and the almost right word" with the difference between "lightning and the lightning bug." He is exaggerating in order to make his point. Unlike more scientific analogies, poetic analogies are not supposed to be very precise. They are just used to illustrate a point.

The Difference between Analogy and Generalization

By now you may be wondering, "What is the difference between an analogy and a generalization?" Actually, they both work on the same principle – when we generalize we are using an analogy, and when we analogize we are using a generalization. This is what distinguishes the two:

Here is a generalization:

EXAMPLE D

"Both Hill Brook College and Valley Knoll College are large colleges. They are both located in conservative towns. They both also happen to be the kind of college you would like to attend. Therefore, all large colleges which are in conservative towns are colleges which you would like to attend."

When we *generalize,* we take a *sample,* then we draw a conclusion about everything in the same class – all large colleges in conservative towns are nice; all blue Fords which have V-8's will be fast; 78% of all salmon patties are infected with E.coli, etc.

Here is an analogy:

EXAMPLE E

"Hill Brook College is a large college. Valley Knoll College is also a large college. Hill Brook is located in a conservative town. Valley Knoll is also located in a conservative town. You know Hill Brook is the kind of college that you would like to attend. Therefore, Valley Knoll is also the kind of college you would like to attend."

When we draw an *analogy* we *compare* items with each other, then we draw a conclusion about one item, based on what we know about the other item – Valley Knoll College will be good because Hill Brook is, Bert's car will be fast because Clyde's is, Mr. Smith will be sick tonight because he was the other nights. We are drawing this conclusion from the *similarities* we have seen between the items we have examined.

Exercises

A. Are these examples analogies, generalizations, or neither?

1. "Curt and Bert are both redheads. They both have freckles. They both live in California. Curt has a really bad temper. Since they are so much alike, Bert must have a bad temper."

2. "All of the cities in Ohio that have a large population and a significant crime problem also have a large police force. Therefore, all large cities that have a significant crime problem also have a large police force."

3. "My cousin, Sylvia, is a redhead and she has a bad temper. My cousin, Albert, on my mother's sister's husband's side, is a redhead, and he has a really bad temper. I'm a redhead and I have a very bad temper. Everybody with red hair must have bad tempers."

4. "My cousin, Sylvia, is a redhead and she has a bad temper. My cousin, Albert, on my mother's sister's husband's side, is a redhead, and he has a really bad temper. I'm a redhead and I have a very bad temper. The grocery store clerk has red hair. He must have a bad temper."

5. "Communism is like prohibition: it's a good idea but it won't work." – Will Rogers

6. "The broad mass of a nation ... will more easily fall victim to a big lie than to a small one." – Adolf Hitler

7. "It seems as if every time I buy a burger at McDonald's it's squashed. I think McDonald's employees always squash their burgers before they serve them. It's probably a company policy."

8. Jenny: "Chimpanzees have a larger brain size than either dolphins or dodos, and dolphins are very smart. Therefore, I think you are dumb because you look like a gorilla."

9. "This thing of being a hero, about the main thing to it is to know when to die." – Will Rogers

10. "A man should keep his little brain attic stocked with all the furniture that he is likely to use, and the rest he can put away in the lumber room of his library, where he can get it if he wants." – Sherlock Holmes

11. "Ex-Professor Moriarty of mathematical celebrity ... is the Napoleon of Crime, Watson." – Sherlock Homes

12. "Let's say you examine 400 engineers all over the world and of that number, 300 have at least 8 pens in their shirt pockets. Therefore, you conclude, 75% of engineers keep at least 8 pens in their shirt pockets."

B. Turn these analogies into generalizations. For example, if the analogy is:
> Yesterday was cloudy and it rained.
> The day before that, it was cloudy and it rained.
> Today is cloudy.
> Conclusion: I think it will rain.

Similar conclusion, but worded as a generalization: "All cloudy days will be rainy days."

13. "The last time it rained, the flowers bloomed.
The time before that, when it rained, the flowers bloomed.
The next time it rains the flowers will bloom."

14. "Texas is a southern state near the ocean and it has palm trees. Florida is a southern state near the ocean and it has palm trees. Louisiana is a southern state near the ocean. I'll bet it has palm trees."

15. "Winning a suit against the government is like getting into a fistfight with Tony. They are so big and mean, you could never win."

Lesson 23

Weak Analogy

So how can we tell if an analogy is strong or weak?

> I. IF THE SIMILARITIES BETWEEN THE ITEMS BEING COMPARED ARE MAJOR AND THE DIFFERENCES ONLY MINOR, THEN IT IS A *strong analogy*.

Let's say, for example, you are a budding scientist wanting to write your graduate thesis on the long term effects of Pop-Tarts on humans. The only problem is, you can't find enough people who are willing to eat thirty-four Pop-Tarts a day for one year. So you decide to do the experiment on some kind of animal, hoping the results will be similar.

You pick orangutans. There are a lot of similarities between orangutans and people, at least as far as basic anatomy goes. (Hans: Well, actually, I have been informed that this is not the case, but we'll assume it, so I don't have to come up with another example.) Let's say we are both about the same size and have generally the same digestive systems – these similarities are relevant to our study. However, there are some differences between orangutans and humans. Orangutans tend to be a little more hairy and have shorter noses than people. Also, people usually don't dip their fingers into the punch bowl at parties.

But, in regard to our experiment, these differences seem minor. The similarities between orangutans and humans are major and the differences probably minor.

If you fed Pop-Tarts to striped cucumber beetles for the proper amount of time, it just wouldn't be the same as if you picked orangutans.

> 2. IF THE DIFFERENCES BETWEEN THE ITEMS BEING COMPARED ARE

MAJOR AND THE SIMILARITIES MINOR, THEN WE CALL IT A *weak analogy*.

Let's go back to Clyde's and Bert's new automobiles. Suppose their conversation went like this:

EXAMPLE A

Clyde: "Our new car is a blue Ford. It has a fifteen-gallon gas tank, five cup holders, and a sun roof. It sure drives fast!"

Bert: "Hey! Our car has all of those things. I'll bet it drives fast too."

Clyde's and Bert's new cars do have many similarities. However, color, size of gas tank, and number of cup holders have little to do with the car's speed on the road. The similarities are only minor. If we found that the two cars differed in ways related to speed – Clyde's car had a large engine and was designed by BMW, while Bert's had a small engine and was made for removing garbage – we might say the differences were major.

The funny thing is, carmakers use this trick on gullible consumers. They take a cheap, underpowered car that can barely accelerate onto the freeway, and give it sleek styling, just like the real sports cars, hoping people will draw a weak analogy between the real sports cars and their car: "Hey, it looks like it could really go fast!"

The fallacy of *weak analogy* is claiming that some items which have only a few minor similarities are practically the same in almost everything else.

Calvin uses a weak analogy. Sparrows and little boys are very different.

Sometimes people come up with very wild analogies.

EXAMPLE B

Clyde: "I think it is all right for governments in developing countries to execute citizens who don't agree with the government."

Jenny: "That sounds terrible! Why do you think they should be allowed to do that?"

Clyde: "Hey, if you want to make an omelet you have to break a few eggs."

Clyde, of course, is being ridiculous. The similarities between a developing nation and cooking breakfast are so minor it would be a waste of time to mention them.

Exercises

A. Here are some analogies with some other relevant, or irrelevant, evidence below each analogy. Does the added evidence strengthen, weaken, or do nothing for the analogy?

"I bought my last three pairs of hiking shoes at Wilson's Shoe Store, and they all lasted a long time. I just bought another pair of hiking shoes at Wilson's Shoe Store. I think this pair will also last a long time."

1. Suppose that the last three pairs of hiking shoes were a different make than the one you are buying now.
2. Suppose that Wilson's Shoe Store was bought out by a larger company recently.
3. Suppose that the last three pairs of hiking shoes are the same brand and kind as the ones you just bought.
4. Suppose that the shoemakers' union was recently on strike.
5. Suppose that you just bought a new puppy who likes to chew shoes.
6. Suppose that Toledo is not the capital of Ohio.
7. Suppose that the last three pairs of shoes were made by Nike, and these new shoes were also made by Nike.
8. Suppose you had the flu when you went into the shoe store, and only *thought* you went into Wilson's.

The three dogs you owned over the last twenty years were German Shepherd dogs. All three of them were very well-behaved, and you were happy with them. Now you have just bought another German Shepherd puppy. You think it will be a nice dog as well.

9. Suppose that the last three dogs were females and this one is also a female.
10. Suppose that the last three dogs were females and this one is a male.
11. Suppose the last three dogs were bought from a different kennel than this new one.
12. Suppose that the last three dogs you owned died before they were three years old.
13. Suppose that you owned the last three dogs when you were very young.
14. Suppose your aunt Martha likes cats better than dogs.
15. Suppose you hate small dogs.
16. Suppose the new dog was trained as an attack dog, while the other three were not.

B. Decide whether the following analogies are, in your opinion, strong or weak.

17. "Chicago and Detroit are cities of approximately the same size. They are both located in the Midwest near a large body of water. I know Chicago has a bad crime problem, so Detroit must also have a bad crime problem."

18. "Rock music is bad for you. I heard a test was done with cows. They had two milk cows listen to music. One listened to Mozart and the other listened to heavy metal. The one that listened to Mozart produced more milk and acted more contented, while the one that listened to heavy metal ate more, knocked over the milk bucket, and grew a horn."

19. "*David Copperfield* was a novel by Charles Dickens, set in England, and I hated it. *Oliver Twist* was a novel by Charles Dickens, set in England, and I hated it. *Great Expectations* is a novel by Charles Dickens, set in England. I think I will hate it."

20. "Since a single human cell becomes a grown man over a period of a few years, then surely it can't be impossible for a single-cell organism to become the human race over a period of several million years."

21. Bert: "You shouldn't put saccharin in your coffee – it's bad for you. Saccharin has been known to cause cancer in lab rats."

22. "I liked *It's a Wonderful Life*, and that movie had James Stewart in it. I liked *Flight of the Phoenix*, and that movie had James Stewart in it. I liked *Mr. Smith Goes to Washington*, and that movie had James Stewart in it. This next movie has James Stewart in it. I think I will like it."

23. "Humor can be dissected, as a frog can, but the thing dies in the process." – E. B. White

24. "Noise proves nothing. Often a hen who has merely laid an egg cackles as if she had laid an asteroid." – Mark Twain

25. "The progress of humanity is like climbing an endless ladder; it
    is impossible to climb higher without first taking the lower steps.
    …Hence it is no accident that the first cultures arose in places
    where the Aryan, in his encounters with lower peoples, subjugated
    them and bent them to his will. They then became the first techni-
    cal instrument in the service of a developing culture." – Adolf
    Hitler in *Mein Kampf*

C. Read the following sections and answer the questions listed below each
one.

"Legal rights for mosquitoes! New studies show that mosquitoes have
a similar genetic makeup to lawyers. Yes, a study conducted by the
American Lawyer Behavior Research Trust (ALBRT) finds that there are
striking similarities between mosquitoes and the common lawyer. And,
yes, you've probably already guessed what they are. It seems mosquitoes
have been found to have an obnoxious propensity towards the sucking
of human blood, a behavioral trait formerly thought to be found only in
leeches and lawyers. Mosquitoes have also been known to carry viruses
and bacteria from host to host, thus contributing to the spread of disease,
an ability long attributed to lawyers who propagate and multiply, leading to a weak and diseased society. 'We believe that mosquitoes are the
closest living ancestors to the modern lawyer…and the differences are
very minor,' says Harry Johnson, Vice President of the American Lawyer
Behavior Research Trust. 'Since lawyers are allowed to practice law, we
think mosquitoes should not be barred from taking the bar exams either.'
'While mosquitoes share approximately 75% of their genetic makeup with
lawyers,' he says, 'the reason we put mosquitoes earlier on the geologic
column is because they are not as developed as lawyers. Mosquitoes aren't
able to get blood out of a turnip,' he states. 'We are currently searching for
the missing link between mosquitoes and lawyers.'"

26. What is being compared here?

27. How does this show that the similarities between the two things
    are major and the differences minor?

28. What conclusion is drawn from this analogy?

29. In your opinion, is this conclusion justified?

"The Great Ape Legal Project (GALP) is a joint project of the Animal Legal Defense Fund and the Great Ape Project International. Its goal is to establish legal rights for nonhuman great apes, including the right to life, liberty and protection from torture…

'…We now have sufficient information about the capacities of great apes to make it clear that the moral boundary we draw between us and them is indefensible,' states Peter Singer, who cofounded the Great Ape Project in 1993. Research by Dr. Roger Fouts, Dr. Jane Goodall and other primatologists has demonstrated that chimpanzees are aware, that they experience pain, and have rich mental and social lives. As individuals they are highly intelligent and have well-developed cognitive skills. They express a broad range of emotions previously thought to be limited to humans – joy, sadness, grief, rage, fear and even a sense of humor. They can reason, plan for the future, make and use tools, be curious and inventive, engage in sophisticated nonverbal communications and learn over 300 signs in American Sign Language. Chimpanzees are our closest biological relatives, sharing 98.4% of our DNA…. Because the similarities between us are so compelling, there is no ethical justification for the difference in legal status." – from the Animal Legal Defense Fund

30. What is being compared here?

31. How does this show that the similarities between the two things are major and the differences minor?

32. What conclusion is drawn from this analogy?

33. In your opinion, is this conclusion justified?

Lesson 24

Post Hoc Ergo Propter Hoc

Post hoc ergo propter hoc is a Latin phrase which means: "after this, therefore, because of this." Apparently, this name was given to this fallacy back when Latin was popular among fallacy detectives. The name has stuck, so we aren't changing it now.

> *Post hoc ergo propter hoc* **is concluding that since A happened before B, then A must have caused B.**

Suppose you live where we do, and it is the middle of February. As usual, it is thirty-two degrees below zero with six and a half feet of snow. You hate cold weather, and wish it was warmer, so you tune in the weatherman on the radio. He says: "Tomorrow the temperature will rise up to a blistering thirty-three degrees." The next day, this happens. The top quarter-inch of snow melts. "Whoa," you gasp. "That weatherman is some guy. First he says it will get warmer, and then it does. The weatherman must have made it warmer." Quickly, you call up the station and ask the weatherman to make it sunny with highs of seventy-eight and lows of seventy-two for the next week.

You have committed the fallacy of *post hoc ergo propter hoc*. You assumed that since the weatherman said it would get warmer *before* it got warmer, the weatherman *caused* it to get warmer.

EXAMPLE B

Three months ago, we were all doing fine – the budget was balanced, the economy was great, we were at peace with other nations and the weather was warm. Then we elected a new president. Since then everything has gone down-hill. Now we have a large budget deficit, the economy is in the pits, we're at war with Antarctica, and it's cold outside. It's obvious that the new president caused all this because he was elected just before all this happened.

If the new president was elected just before everything went bad, that doesn't necessarily mean the new president caused it to go bad. This is a common error in reasoning. We see something happen, good or bad, then look for what happened just before it – expecting to find the cause. But what happened just before it is often not the cause.

If we trip and sprain an ankle we will think of all the "unlucky" things that happened that day – we saw a black cat, walked under a ladder, or opened an umbrella in the house. We superstitiously conclude that these unrelated things caused the sprained ankle, because they happened before it.

EXAMPLE C

Father: "Son, I think this electric guitar you bought is influencing you for the worse."

Son: "Uh, why dude … er … Dad?"

Father: "Ever since you bought it, you have been growing your hair longer and have been slouching around the house with your hands in your pockets. We have also noticed that you have spoken more disrespectfully to your mother and me, and you haven't been doing as much housework."

This father is committing the *post hoc ergo propter hoc* fallacy. He concludes that since the electric guitar was bought just before the bad behavior, the electric guitar caused the bad behavior. While the electric guitar may be causing the bad behavior, it is also possible that a general decline in his son's morals is causing both the buying of the electric guitar and the long hair, slouching, disrespectfulness, and laziness. Maybe his son is hanging out with the wrong crowd.

Sometimes a *post hoc ergo propter hoc* is true – what happened before *is* the cause. When an egg breaks on a concrete floor, it seems logical to think immediately of what you did just before it broke – you dropped it, so that was the cause. However, if A happened before B, we don't have enough reason to conclude immediately that A caused B – we need to find out a bit more.

Exercises

A. For these examples of *post hoc ergo propter hoc*, give some other, possibly overlooked, causes for the events in question.

1. "I've been looking into the history of wars. It seems as if, just before any war, all the countries involved build large armies. I think that the building of a large army causes war."

2. "These shoes are my best shoes. They help me to pass tests. The last three times I wore them was on test days, and I passed the tests."

B. Name the faulty reasoning, if any, in the following exercises.

3. "Religion is a waste of time and energy, because there's no reason to spend our lives in prayer when we all have better things to do."

4. "Yesterday I was painting a room. I was up on a ladder when I decided it needed to be moved. I climbed down and, not thinking about what I was doing, walked under the ladder. Just when I realized this was unlucky, I tripped over a black cat which was under the ladder, then fell over and smashed the mirror which I was about to install. Now do you understand why I have two broken legs, and my house was repossessed?"

5. Person in Post Office: "The United States is the most powerful nation today, and you work for the powerful U.S. government as a mailman here in the Wichiwachi Post Office. So, don't tell me you don't know where my package went to – all the forces of western civilization are arrayed on your side!"

6. "Communist governments always end in failure. Look what happened to the Soviet Union."

7. Mrs.: "My head hurts. I think these pills are giving me headaches."
    Mr.: "Why do you think that, honey?"
    Mrs.: "Because it says 'may cause headaches' right here on the bottle."

8. "A cloud is 90% water, a watermelon is 90% water. Therefore, since a plane can fly through a cloud, a plane can fly through a watermelon."

9. "Ever since Clyde started cozying up with the teacher and talking really nice to her, he has been getting A's and B's. It's very obvious that he is now the teacher's pet. I think it's unfair."

10. Young Bachelor: "Either I marry her and she drives me crazy with all her talking, or I don't marry her and I go crazy the rest of my life thinking about her."

11. Jenny: "Meat is very bad for you. You should never eat it. It rots in your stomach."
Bert: "How do you know that?"
Jenny: "Well, it takes over twenty-four hours to digest meat. Why don't you just take a piece of bacon and set it out in the driveway for twenty-four hours and see what it smells like afterward. Yuck!"

12. Political Candidate A: "I think the federal government has no business in education."
Political Candidate B: "So you don't think it is a national priority then?"

13. Farmer McDonald: "Ever since they put up that new power plant across the river, we haven't had a bit of rain. I'm tellin' you, mankind has got too big for its britches when it fiddles around with nature."

14. "Are you reading the book *The Fallacy Detective*? Isn't that book about logic? Logic is evil. The first person we know who talked about logic was Aristotle, and he was a pagan."

15. Larry was a kind, gentle man. He always spoke softly and was kind to his wife. Then his wife started to buy crunchy instead of creamy peanut butter. Soon, Larry showed signs of being easily irritated. His voice sounded gruff and he was rude to the neighbors. When Larry's wife noticed this, she went around the house and threw out all of the crunchy peanut butter.

16. Bert: "My pastor knows a lot about the Bible. He has been to seminary and he knows Greek. He says baptism should always be done by immersion. He must be right."
Clyde: "My pastor also knows a lot about the Bible. He has been to seminary, he knows Greek, and he even knows Hebrew too. I'll bet your pastor doesn't know Hebrew. My pastor believes in baptism by sprinkling. My pastor must be right and yours wrong – mine knows Hebrew and yours doesn't."

17. Elder and Wiser Brother: "Some Congressman pled the Fifth in court today. Have you learned what they mean by "pled the Fifth?"
Little Sister: "I think it means the Fifth Amendment to the Constitution.
Elder and Wiser Brother: "And what is the Fifth Amendment about?
Little Sister: "Temporary insanity?"

18. "If you think we are too secluded in this town, why don't you go commit a crime and go to prison. I'll bet you meet some pretty varied people in there."

19. Jenny: "You can't just steal that!"
Shoplifter: "Why not? They do it in baseball all the time."

Lesson 25

Post Hoc Ergo Propter Hoc in Statistics

We have all heard people tell us:

EXAMPLE A

"Young man, you want to make plenty of money when you grow up, don't you? Well, you need to attend the best college you can afford. Studies have shown, the better the college you go to, the more money you make later in life."
– A Concerned Friend

Your concerned friend is only thinking of your future happiness. He thinks going to a good college will make you richer. He thinks his advice is backed up with hard, cold evidence – and it is – it's only the interpretation he gets all wrong.

Your concerned friend has probably seen a study similar to this one:

A prominent college, like Harvard, will look up all the people who graduated about twenty years before, and survey them – how much money they are making, what kind of a job they have, etc. The results confirm what they thought. The average Harvard graduate makes $75,000 a year and has a condo in Palm Beach. They will then compare this with the numbers from similar studies done by less prominent colleges, and, bang! Harvard graduates make more money.

"I can't argue with the numbers," you say. "Then you can't argue with the conclusion," they say. "Attending Harvard College will make you a rich man! Right?" … Wrong.

Enter *post hoc ergo propter hoc*. If the average Harvard graduate makes more money *after* attending Harvard, that doesn't mean he is making more money *because* he attended Harvard. And, incidentally, if *you* attend Harvard, *you* aren't necessarily going to be rich either.

"Then how do you explain these hard cold facts? Why do Harvard graduates make more money if it isn't because they went to Harvard?" they ask.

The reality may show a different picture. The teenagers who attend prestigious colleges, like Harvard, are usually one of two types: those who have a lot of brains and those who have rich parents. The smart ones would probably end up making plenty of money whether they attended Harvard or went somewhere else, and the rich kids are probably going to end up making plenty of money because their parents did – money breeds money.

So, there really is no cold hard evidence to show you that if you attend Harvard you will end up making more money.

A and B don't have to actually follow each other in time to be a *post hoc ergo propter hoc* – they can both happen at the same time. This fallacy is also being committed when somebody says that since A and B are commonly seen together, one must have caused the other.

EXAMPLE B

> A recent study by the New England Association of Connection Concocters finds that there is a great difference in test scores between people who listen to classical music and people who listen to more popular music. People who normally listen to at least fifteen minutes of classical music a day scored many points higher on standardized tests than people who normally listened to heavy metal. Those who listened to country scored the lowest. The report says, "These results have far-reaching ramifications for our everyday life. Music has a far greater power on our basic functions than we ever thought." – Something Hans Made Up

Look out for their "obvious" conclusion: if you want to score higher on a test, break out the Mozart. And, to carry it a step further, heavy metal makes you dumb. If classical music and good grades are seen together, then the classical music must have *caused* the good grades. We all want this to be true – it even seems logical. But why couldn't it be the other way around? The people who do well on tests are smarter and tend to have a better taste in music and listen to classical, and those who tend to do worse on tests listen to heavy metal and country.

EXAMPLE C

Does failing to brush your teeth encourage you to kill yourself? A recent study, conducted over the past fifty years, has revealed a relationship between toothbrush sales and suicide rates. Whenever toothbrush sales in the U.S. drop, the suicide rate climbs. Also, when people start to buy more toothbrushes, there are fewer suicides. "This is astounding," says the president of Colgate. "We have always recommended that people brush their teeth, but we never thought it was this important."– Another Thing Hans Made Up

People draw wild connections between things which would normally appear to be totally unrelated. This example could be a case where an overlooked cause is masterminding both things. The economy takes a dive and people don't have enough money to buy new toothbrushes. And, people kill themselves because their businesses aren't doing too well – also a result of the bad economy.

Exercises

A. What form of faulty reasoning, if any, is being used in the following exercises?

1. Jenny: "You know jaywalking is against the law, don't you?"
   Bert: "And I suppose you never jaywalked in your life?"

2. "I heard Candidate Schwartz say that he wasn't a Democrat, so he must be running on the Republican ticket."

3. Mr.: "I've changed my mind. I've decided to not marry you."
   Miss: "But we've been planning on getting married all afternoon."
   Mr.: "Well, I know, but I heard most suicides are committed in June. We all know that most weddings are in June. Marriage must drive guys to suicide. I don't want to get depressed and kill myself."

4. Mr.: "Well, maybe I will marry you."
   Miss: "What! Why are you changing your mind again?"
   Mr.: "I heard somewhere else that married people live longer than unmarried people. I don't want to die young."
   Miss: "That's it. Just forget the whole thing. I'm not going to marry such a fickle guy. All you care about is yourself."

5. "Studies have shown that people who exercise several times a week have a lower chance of heart disease. You should exercise. It certainly won't do you any harm, and it might do you some good."

6. Jenny: "I think I'm going to become a vegetarian. It will make me healthier."
   Bert: "Why? How do you know it will make you healthier?"
   Jenny: "Because I read somewhere that vegetarians are healthier than the average American.

7. Government Report: "A low income level seems to be the greatest factor contributing to why some families, where both parents work full time, are still below the poverty line."

8. "A few years ago, they raised the speed limit in this state to 75 miles per hour, and now we have a higher accident rate. I think the higher speed limit is causing more accidents – if people are driving faster, they can't control their vehicles as well, and this results in more accidents."

9. "Babe Ruth always used Louisville Sluggers whenever he went up to bat. He said they were the best bats around. All the New York Yankees used them in fact. I think I'll buy one."

10. "Our rooster crows every morning. Then the sun comes up. Now do you understand how important roosters are?"

11. "I have argued with my pastor three times in the last month. Each time, he gets angry and those little veins in his forehead stick out. Therefore, anytime anybody argues with him he will get angry and those little veins will stick out."

12. Child: "Who made God?"

13. Father: "What is that? You have a tattoo!"
Son: "Ah, Dad, it's only a bunny."
Father: "Don't you know that all the people in prison have tattoos. I don't want you to end up there."

14. "Sleeping for too long is bad for your health. Researchers have found that those who sleep for longer than seven hours a night have a much higher death rate. This six-year study analyzed the sleeping patterns of over a million adults who were over thirty years old. These researchers found that those who slept eight hours a night were 12% more likely to die within six years. Those who slept five hours a night lived longer than those who slept more than eight hours."

B. Read this and answer the questions below it.
"A gun in your home does not make you safer. Even though the National Rifle Association claims that you need a gun in your home to protect you and your family from home invasion, research shows that the person most likely to shoot you or a family member with your gun already lives with you. According to a study by the *New England Journal of Medicine*, guns kept in the home for self-protection are twenty-two times more likely to be used to kill someone you know, rather than to be used in self-defense."
– Paraphrased from something off the Internet

15. What is the conclusion in this quotation?

16. How does it define "someone you know?"

17. How would the researchers know if a gun was kept for self-protection?

18. What do the authors of this quotation imply is the cause-and-effect relationship between owning a gun and people dying?

19. What evidence do they use to show this?

20. What other cause-and-effect scenarios, which are equally possible, can you think of?

Lesson 26

Proof by Lack of Evidence

The *proof by lack of evidence* fallacy is claiming something is true simply because nobody has yet given any evidence to the contrary.

EXAMPLE A

Master Torturer: "Confess! It was you who said the King looked like a platypus."

Accused: "No!"

Master Torturer: "All right Tony, start tickling him."

Accused: "No! Hehe…I…hehehe…didn't…hehe…say…hehe…it…hehe…gasp!"

Master Torturer: "But you must have said it. You haven't yet given us any proof that you didn't say it.…Tickle him some more, Tony."

This torturer's reasoning is wrong. How could the accused give the torturer any evidence that he *didn't* say something?

When someone makes an assertion – "you are guilty of this crime" – that person is the one who is obliged to back it up with evidence – "you are guilty of this crime because I saw you do it." Saying, "you are guilty because you haven't shown me you aren't" would be very lazy reasoning. It shifts the burden of proof onto the accused, when the accuser should have the burden of proving his accusation.

The person who makes an assertion is the one who must prove it. Let's take a look at an assertion.

EXAMPLE B

Bert: "There are mountain lions living in Illinois."

This assertion needs to be backed up with evidence.

> Bert: "I think there are mountain lions living in Illinois."
> Jenny: "Yah, right. Prove it."
> Bert: "Just look behind you."
> Jenny: "Heeeeellllllllp!"

This evidence is good. However, if Bert said:

> Bert: "There must be mountain lions living in Illinois, because I haven't seen any proof that there aren't any."

This would be committing the proof by lack of evidence fallacy. He can't claim that mountain lions live in Illinois only because there isn't any evidence to the contrary. This fallacy works the same for the opposite assertion.

> Jenny: "There are no mountain lions living in Illinois."
> Bert: "How do you know that?"
> Jenny: "Well, prove to me there are some."

This is also the proof by lack of evidence fallacy. Just because no one has seen any mountain lions in Illinois, that doesn't mean we can say for sure there are none – they may hide very well. Jenny is the one who needs to prove what she claims.

> Jenny: "There are no mountain lions in Illinois because I have just examined every square inch of Illinois simultaneously and there were none."

Examining every inch of Illinois simultaneously would be difficult – but it would do the trick.

People make some very imaginative claims using the proof by lack of evidence fallacy.

EXAMPLE C

> Tour Guide: "And now I will show you the famous statue called *The Thinker*. Legend has it that at night *The Thinker* comes down from his post and walks

around the city. But nobody ever sees him. He's so fast he can run back to his post quicker than the blink of an eye."

   Not-So-Gullible Tourist: "Ha! That's the most ridiculous bunch of baloney I've ever heard. How could you prove that?"

   Tour Guide: "But sir, how do you know it *isn't* true?"

Since there is no real way to prove this claim is true, the tour guide must use the proof by lack of evidence fallacy.

Proof by lack of evidence

Not Proof by Lack of Evidence

In a court of criminal law, the burden of proof is always on the accuser – the one who says "that man committed a crime." The accuser can never say: "That man is guilty because he can't prove he didn't do it." Unfortunately, in many courtrooms of the past, innocent people were punished because this was allowed – just like our first example. But, in a courtroom today, an accused person is assumed innocent until proven guilty. In a courtroom, an accused person can rightfully say: "I am innocent because you can't prove me guilty." This is not the proof by lack of evidence fallacy because, in a courtroom, the burden of proof is always on the accuser.

Exercises

A. Which attorney is committing the proof by lack of evidence fallacy?

1. Prosecuting Attorney: "The defense in this case has not given one shred of evidence that the accused was not at the scene of the crime at the time of the murder. They have not given one shred of evidence that the accused is not a homicidal maniac. They have not given one shred of evidence that the accused was not strong enough to kill the victim. In the light of these facts, how can you, the jury, acquit this man?"

Defense attorney: "The prosecution in this case has not presented to us a single proof that my client was at the scene of the crime at the time of the murder. They have not shown us that my client had any murderous intentions. They have not even shown that my client had enough strength to commit the crime. I must insist that my client is innocent."

B. What form of faulty reasoning, if any, is used in the following exercises?

2. Torturer: "You are a heretic. You can't prove that you aren't one, so you are a heretic. Confess, or we will stretch your body out until you are a foot taller."
   Accused: "Ha, you did it – you committed a fallacy! I learned all about it in a book called *The Fallacy Detective*."
   Torturer: "That's enough cheek out of you. Brutus, give the wheel another turn."

3. "The Ford Zip automobile is the safest car to drive. An independent test laboratory placed 200 three-toed tree frogs in 200 Ford Zips, then crashed the cars. Every single frog lived through the crashes and, in fact, seemed to act happier afterward."

4. "The reports of my death are greatly exaggerated." – Mark Twain

5. "My friend, John, is insane. He doesn't look like it, but he's madder than a March Hare. He may look perfectly normal on the outside, but you never know when he'll up and do something crazy. Yep, deep down, he's a raving lunatic. Now, you may ask, how do I know this? Well, can you prove to me that he is sane? I'll bet you can't."

6. Interviewer: "What do you think should be done about people who swear in public?"
   Man On Street: "I think it should be against the law."
   Interviewer: "Oh, I suppose you're against the right to free speech then?"

7. "I've visited France, and I know that the French are a very sophisticated and artistic people. That's why I trust that you, Mr. Arnot, will be able to design my granddaughter's birthday cake as a perfection of culinary delight."

8. Son to Father: "Dad, a family is like a nation in many ways. They both are a group of people related to each other in some way, and they both are an independent entity. Since we all know that a nation works best when it is a democracy, I think we should hold an election to see who will make the decisions around here."

9. "The Bible talks about Hittites, but nowhere in archaeology has there been found any evidence that those people ever existed. Therefore, they never existed and the Bible is in error."

10. Politician: "My fellow voters, I know you are either among the arrogant rich, the lazy poor, or one of the contented middle class like me."

11. Advertisement: "You can buy the new Sensitivity perfume, or you can smell bad all day."

12. Patient: "Doctor, I've been having these urges to go out and rob a bank lately. Should I be worried about this?"
S. Freud: "I don't think so. You see these urges come from your evolutionary past. The survival of the fittest dictates that we try to gain an advantage over other life forms by destroying their means of living. Robbing the bank destroys other people's means of living and helps you to survive. Your desires are just outworkings of the epic struggle for survival."

13. "America is on the brink of an economic depression. Pretty soon all the businesses we think are stable will go bankrupt. We have hard times ahead of us. I see no way around it. After all, how can you show me that things are going to continue forever to be as hunky-dory as they have been. You can't."

14. "There can be nothing wrong with price-fixing. I am sure everybody will agree that a store clerk has the right to fix the prices as he chooses."

15. "Christianity came along in the first century, and a few hundred years after that, the Roman Empire fell. Christianity must have made it fall."

16. "There's no point in listening to you. Everybody knows you're just a little do-gooder."

17. Clyde: "The Jewish Holocaust must have been all right."
Jenny: "That is terrible! You think it was all right for the Germans to try to exterminate the Jews?"
Clyde: "It must have been all right. If the German leaders purposed it, and all the German people approved of it and carried it out, I can't see how they could all have been misguided."

18. "My brother sucked on his thumb until he was ten years old, and now he is a serial killer. Never let your children suck on their thumbs!"

19. "You can't prove you didn't steal the car, so you must be guilty."

20. Farmer McDonald: "I've been lookin' at them rich farmers. I've been tryin' to find out what makes 'em rich.
Farmer Brown: "What did you find out?"
Farmer McDonald: "Every one of them rich farmers has a brand new John Deere tractor. I think that is what makes 'em rich. I'm gonna buy myself one of them John Deere tractors."

21. A recent study has linked the current civil war in Angola with rainfall in the fertile valleys of California. Ever since the civil war in Angola broke out, California has had only small amounts of rainfall. "This is terrible. I don't have half the crop I had ten years ago," says Hank Junior, a kiwi farmer in central California. "Somebody needs to go to Africa and tell those people that their actions affect more people than they think."

22. "There is a God. Nobody has ever come up with any conclusive evidence that there isn't one."

23. Farmer McDonald: "I just returned from my visit to California. Boy, they sure have some high mountains over there. One was over fourteen thousand feet high."

24. Floyd was a poor country boy, but he wanted to be a rich man. He spent much of his time trying to figure out what made people rich. He drove through rich neighborhoods, visited rich relatives, read books by rich authors, and watched "Who Wants to be a Millionaire?" over and over, seeking for a clue to what makes people rich. Then one day, he put it all together. Eureka! Every rich man he knew wore a silk tie. Everybody in the rich neighborhoods wore silk ties when they went off to work; his rich uncle wore a silk tie to all those fancy parties; all the back covers of those rich authors' books sported pictures of them with silk ties; even Regis Philbin wore a silk tie. "This must be it," Floyd said as he went off to Macy's to make his purchase.

25. "It says here in the Bible that God cannot repent. But then it says here that God can repent. This doesn't make any sense to me. Nobody has explained how this isn't a contradiction, so it must be a contradiction."

26. In another recent study, researchers have discovered an astounding fact. Auto accidents tend to rise when people eat more cabbage. Yes, that's right. Researchers have been studying the connection between the consumption of cabbage for people over eighteen and their driving history. "It seems, when people eat more cabbage, they are more often in motor accidents, and when they eat less cabbage, they are often in fewer accidents," says one researcher. "These are intriguing results. We don't know what to do with them."

27. "I have studied science for fifty years and I have never seen a shred of evidence that there is a God. God doesn't exist."

28. "God did not create the world six thousand years ago, because matter has always existed, and therefore the world has always existed."

29. Senator: "I don't think we need to talk to the people in the Justice Department about the practicality of enforcing this bill. The Justice Department is full of Republicans, and so they are already biased against it."

6

Propaganda

HELLO, ABC NEWS? I'VE DISCOVERED AN ANTI-GRAVITY FORMULA.

WHAT?! IT'S NOT NEWSWORTHY?!

TELL HIM IT LETS YOU LOSE WEIGHT WITHOUT EXERCISING.

ISN'T THAT MISLEADING AND UNETHICAL?

THERE'S A FINE LINE BETWEEN MARKETING AND GRAND THEFT.

© 1991 United Feature Syndicate, Inc.

Lesson 27

What Is Propaganda?

Advertisers are always looking for ways to pressure us to buy their products. Manufacturers design everything from automobiles to bars of soap in ways which make them appear irresistible.

EXAMPLE A

"Buy Swiss Springtime soap – it makes you feel all clean and fresh!"

Manufacturers make their automobiles look more tough, more luxurious, or more trendy – all in a race to make us buy.

EXAMPLE B

"BMW: The ultimate driving machine."

In the court room, lawyers give the jury more and more reasons to side with them in the case.

EXAMPLE C

"This criminal is so low, he would steal from his own mother!"

These are all examples of propaganda.

Propaganda **is any strategy for spreading our beliefs or ideas.**

Propaganda can be found in a political speech, a television show, an advertisement, and many other places. Propagandists use many different methods to spread their ideas. We call these propaganda techniques.

Propaganda is not always bad. There is nothing necessarily wrong with spreading our ideas and encouraging people to buy our product – as long as we do it honestly. Unfortunately, sometimes the reasons people give us to buy their product, vote for their candidate, or to do what they want aren't very good. Sometimes these reasons are based on emotions and not on clear thinking. A truck dealer will pressure us to buy his truck because it *looks* tougher – not because it necessarily *is* tougher. The lawyer in the court room will pressure the jury to *feel* that his side is the fair one – not to *know* his side is the fair one.

Our emotions are sometimes correct, but they are often incorrect. It is usually best to think through a matter and not do something just because we feel like doing it.

PEANUTS reprinted by permission of United Feature Syndicate, Inc.

Manipulative propaganda is used when someone plays with our emotions in a way designed to make us agree with them without thinking through the matter carefully. In this chapter, when we discuss propaganda, we mean manipulative propaganda.

When two different propagandists manipulate our emotions in different ways, we often can't decide which emotion to follow.

EXAMPLE D

Defense Attorney: "Ladies and gentlemen of the jury, I urge you to acquit John Jones of this crime of murder. He is married and has three children. If he is executed or goes to prison for life, his family will end up in the poorhouse."

Prosecuting Attorney: "Ladies and gentlemen of the jury, I urge you to convict John Jones of this crime of murder. We need to put him where he can never commit any crimes. If you don't convict him, you may be his next victim."

Notice how both these arguments sound very convincing when you first look at them? The only problem is, you can't take both sides – one side, at least, must be wrong.

Two propaganda techniques are used in this example. Both Defense Attorney and Prosecuting Attorney are manipulating the jury with emotions. One wants them to side with him out of pity, and the other wants them to side with him out of fear.

Neither attorney addresses the real issue – the issue that the jury is supposed to decide: whether John Jones actually commited the murder.

Manipulative propaganda avoids the important issues that should be addressed; it attacks an irrelevant target: our emotions.

When we think we are being manipulated by propaganda, it is useful to ask ourselves: Is this person actually proving what he is saying? Or is he merely making me feel like he has proven it to me? Is what he is saying relevant?

What Is Wrong with Propaganda?

The Bible says that we are supposed to go beyond appearances.

> "Do not judge according to appearance,
> but judge with righteous judgment."
> –John 7:24

We need to scratch a little deeper than our emotions and appearances. We need to determine matters with righteous reasoning.

Propagandists use many different techniques. A few of them are covered in this chapter.

NUNA & TOODLES

Exercises

A. Answer the following questions:

1. What kinds of people use propaganda?

2. Do only bad people use propaganda?

3. What are some places where we hear propaganda?

4. Is it always wrong to use propaganda?

5. Are the viewpoints of propagandists always wrong?

6. Is propaganda always manipulative?

7. Does propaganda always play on our emotions?

8. Is propaganda always irrelevant?

9. Does propaganda always lie?

10. What is the capital of Australia?

B. Which of the following advertisements are using manipulative and emotional propaganda techniques?

11. "There is no God! The majority of Americans believe there is no God!"

12. "Sophisticated and intelligent people believe there is no God."

13. "Only underdeveloped people believe in a God. Religion is only an evolutionary hangover."

14. "God does not exist because I can prove it!"

15. "Wouldn't you feel bad if you believed all your life that there was a God, and then you found out when you died that there wasn't one?"

16. "There is no God!...Thump!...There is no God!...Thump, thump!...There is no God! Thump, thump, thump!...There is no God!...Thump, thump, thump, thump!"

Lesson 28

Appeal to Fear

Appeal to fear is a propaganda technique. *Appeal to fear* is used when some-one makes you fear the consequences of not doing what he wants.
Let's go back to the example we gave in the last lesson:

EXAMPLE A

Prosecuting Attorney: "Ladies and gentlemen of the jury, I urge you to con-vict John Jones of this crime of murder. We need to put him where he can never commit any crimes. If you don't convict him, you may be his next victim."

This statement does not address the proper question: did John Jones actually commit this murder? Instead, the prosecuting attorney is trying to disturb the jury with the fear of being murdered: "I need to convict this man whether he is guilty or not; I may be his next victim!" This reasoning, of course, is illogical.

It is never good to act out of fear. However, fear is a strong motivator. When people fear something, they tend to not think matters through. They think out of cringe-reflex. "Help! Something bad could happen!"

Appeal to fear is used in commercials like this one:

EXAMPLE B

Advertisement: A picture of a dingy bathroom. A voice says, "Is this what your bathroom looks like?" This is followed by a microscopic close-up of the bathtub, showing little bugs crawling around. "Here is what is going on where you can't see." "Use Everclean for a fresher looking bathroom."

This advertisement wants us to dread the thought of little bugs crawling around in our bathrooms (whether or not they do any real damage), and then, hopefully, buy their product.

When the person appealing to fear is actually the one dealing out the fear, the situation can take on a more brutal form.

EXAMPLE C

Restaurant Owner: "You no lika da pizzas? I send over my cousin Tony for a little change a' mind. He maka you lika da pizzas."

This can be very effective. When someone fears something or someone, he often makes decisions which he might not make in calmer situations. If big-fisted Tony is across from us, we might think it wiser to decide we like the pizza after all – no matter how many anchovies are on it.

EXAMPLE D

"The Nazis used to send the following notice to German readers who let their subscriptions lapse: 'Our paper certainly deserves the support of every German. We shall continue to forward copies of it to you, and hope that you will not want to expose yourself to unfortunate consequences in the case of cancellation.'"
– *Parade Magazine*, May 9, 1971

This style of persuasion can be very effective. We would want to renew our subscriptions, even if we didn't like the magazine.

PEANUTS reprinted by permission of United Feature Syndicate, Inc.

Linus is persuaded by an appeal to fear.

The fear of physical harm is not the only "force" in question.

EXAMPLE E

"If this Supreme Court continues to wade into this thicket and make substantive rulings on behalf of George Bush, this court will go down in history as the most interventionist court ever in deciding a political matter." – Tom Harkin, Senator from Iowa

There is no logical argument here. Tom Harkin is urging the Supreme Court to make a ruling out of fear that history would look back disapprovingly upon them later – not a ruling based on who is correct.

Not an Appeal to Fear

An appeal to fear is not being used when somebody threatens us but doesn't try to change our opinion.

EXAMPLE F

Bank Robber: "If you don't transfer all of the money into my account, I will give you a bad case of lead poisoning with this gun here."

This is not an appeal to fear because the robber is not trying to change our minds, he is just giving us our options – do what he says or die. Of course, sometimes there is a fine line between an appeal to fear and a mere threat. But, for us, an appeal to fear is trying to change someone's opinion out of fear of something. A threat is just offering someone a choice between doing what we want or suffering the consequences.

"The fear of man brings a snare,
  but whoever trusts in the Lord shall be safe."
–Proverbs 29:25

Exercises

Which of the following examples are an appeal to fear?

1. An advertisement for a new car with improved brakes: Scene of a mother driving the new car with young daughter sleeping in the passenger seat. Suddenly, a deer jumps in front of the car. The screen freezes. A voice says: "Does your car have antilock brakes?"

2. "Chevy Suburban. Like a Rock."

3. "Do you know what kind of damage a loose cow can do on your farm? Imagine what would happen if your electric fence failed and your cows wandered into the neighbor's field. Buy a 'Zapper' electric fence and you won't have to worry about it."

4. C.E.O.: "Before we begin this board meeting – where we will be deciding some important things – I would like to remind you who is the boss, and who can fire you."

5. Parent: "I hope you agree with me that my little Johnny did well on that last test – I contribute a lot of money to this school."

6. "Everybody put your money in this bag, or my cousin Vern, over here, will sing 'The Star-Spangled Banner' really loud!"

7. "Mothers of River City, heed that warning before it's too late. Watch for the telltale signs of corruption [from the pool table]: the minute your son leaves the house, does he re-buckle his knickerbockers below the knee? Is there a nicotine stain on his index finger? A dime novel hidden in the corncrib? Is he startin' to memorize jokes from *Capn' Billie's Whizbang*? Are certain words creeping into his conversation? Words like: 'swell' and 'so's your ole man.' Well, if so my friends, you got trouble." – Professor Harold Hill in *The Music Man*

8. "Disperse, you rebels!"

9. "Disperse, you rebels, or we will fire!"

10. "I hope you see the reasonableness of dispersing – remember who has the most guns."

Lesson 29

Appeal to Pity

When someone tries to make us do something only because we pity him, or we pity something associated with him, he is using the propaganda technique called *appeal to pity*.

EXAMPLE A

Radio advertisement: "Mr. Jones lost the last election because his opponent used a smear campaign to discredit him. Mr. Jones lost the election before that because of voter fraud. Mr. Jones lost the election before that because nobody knew who he was. Don't you think it is about time you voted for Mr. Jones?"

Poor Mr. Jones. But, wait a minute, this advertisement doesn't give us any real reasons why Mr. Jones would make a good officeholder.

EXAMPLE B

Officer: "I stopped you because you were going 58 miles per hour in a 25 mile-per-hour zone. I'm going to have to write you a ticket."
Motorist: "But officer, this is the fifth ticket I've been given this year. If I get another ticket, then they will take my license away, and I won't be able to drive to work. My wife and children will starve."

The motorist may be in a predicament, but his point is irrelevant. The very fact that he has received five tickets in one year probably means he doesn't care enough about his family to drive safely – especially when his job is on the line. This motorist is attempting to manipulate the officer by appealing to his pity.

EXAMPLE C

"After a debate touching on their own four-legged friends, senators [of the California senate] voted to forbid condominiums and mobile home parks from completely banning pets.

Supporters said the bill would help many Californians, including older residents, whose lives could be brightened by animals.

Arguing for the bill, Senate leader John Burton, D-San Francisco, recalled that his own mother was greatly comforted by her little dog after Burton's father passed away.

'That poodle was a companion of my mother, who naturally, after the death of my father, was living at home alone,' Burton said." – *The Sacramento Bee*, August 23, 2000

This is an old trick. An anecdote about our mother being comforted in her old age by little Fu-Fu is not the point. She may not even live in a condominium. The supporters of this bill want us to pity the people who live in condos and then vote for the law. They don't want us to think about whether or not the government has any right to become involved.

Sometimes an appeal to pity tries to make us feel guilty.

EXAMPLE D

"Every year, millions of people around the world build new homes, and put groceries in bags made out of trees taken from the Amazon rain forests. This destroys habitat for endangered animals, making it difficult for these poor animals to live. It is estimated that this rate of destruction of rain forest causes the extinction of 12 species of animal every 65.944 seconds. Don't you think you should do something about this?"

Doesn't this appeal make you feel at least a little guilty? Is the issue really that simple?

Appeal to pity

Exercises

What form of propaganda, if any, is being used?

1. Credit card advertisement: Picture of a shark attacking. "Free card replacement if lost, stolen, or devoured."

2. "Gun manufacturers should do something about all those guns we have lying around. My grandson was brutally murdered last summer by another child with a gun."

3. Car advertisement of bright-colored sports sedan: "It's friendly and loves to play."

4. "Teacher, please give me a passing grade. If I don't pass, my dad says I can't leave the house for a month."

5. "Could you please give me a little money? I am in trouble – our house just burnt down, the car was just repossessed, I lost my job, my whole family has pneumonia, and the Mafia has a price on my head."

6. "Could you please give me a little money? I am in trouble – our house just burnt down, the car was just repossessed, I lost my job, my whole family has pneumonia, the Mafia has a price on my head, and I lost all my money to a robber."

7. "Kansas Gov. Bill Graves, a Republican, warned [Kansas school] board members not to adopt [some] anti-evolution curriculum, and has said he would support an effort to abolish the Board of Education." – From the MSNBC website.

8. Mrs.: "I need a diamond ring."
   Mr.: "Why? You already have lots of jewelry."
   Mrs.: "Sniff, sniff, but, sniff, I just want to have something, sniff, to make me feel, sniff, better."

9. Advertisement: "Sweet and Smooth cigarettes."

10. Criminal: "But judge, if you convict me, I'll be branded for life. When I get out, nobody will want me to work for them."

11. "Help! Our house is on fire and my infant son is still inside. Can you please help us?"

12. Advertisement: "Should your kids have to worry about nuclear war?"

Lesson 30

Bandwagon

When advertisements and articles encourage us to "join the millions," the propaganda technique of bandwagon is being used. Teenagers often want to do "what everybody else is doing."

EXAMPLE A

Clyde: "Dad, can I go to see the movie 'Attack of the Killer Wombats'?"
Dad: "No, son, you can't go. I heard that movie has bad things in it."
Clyde: "Aw, come on, everybody's going to see it."

Clyde is using a bandwagon on his dad.

The bandwagon technique invites us to jump on the bandwagon and do what everybody else is doing. This technique pressures us to do something just because many other people like us are doing it.

EXAMPLE B

"More Americans get their news from ABC than from any other source."

Just because more Americans get their news from ABC, does that necessarily mean that ABC gives us the best news?
This propaganda technique is the reason why parents frequently ask their children:

Mom: "If (friend's name is inserted here) jumped off a cliff, would you?"
Son: "Of course. Where's the cliff?"

If all the people in the world are doing something – like going to a particular movie, wearing a particular style of clothing, or believing a particular teaching – that isn't enough reason for us to do it also.

EXAMPLE C

"This year, over 117,574 people will visit the Virgin Islands."

Bandwagon has a lot to do with peer pressure. Everybody has an incredible urge inside them to do what their peers are doing. Most of the time we know it is wrong, but we do it anyway.

You shall not follow a crowd to do evil;
    nor shall you testify in a dispute
    so as to turn aside after many to pervert justice.
–Exodus 23:2

The issue is not whether everybody else does it. The issue is whether it is right or wrong. Is that movie a good movie to go to? Is this news source more reliable?

Exercises

What form of propaganda, if any, is being used in the following exercises?

1. Constituent standing in front of senator: "Senator, I have walked all the way from Claremore, Oklahoma, barefoot, just to tell you not to vote for Senate Bill 254."

2. Mr.: "I think we need to buy a new car.
   Mrs.: "Why? Our car is only a few years old, and we haven't had any problems with it yet."
   Mr.: "I think it is a good idea to buy a new car. It would make us look better to our neighbors. The Smiths just bought a new Cadillac, and the what's-their-names just bought a new Ford station wagon."

3. "All evidence points to those hoarding specific products as being a small minority who are overreacting to the issue of y2k." – The Tasmanian State Government discouraging panic buying.

4. Picture of a man knocking down the Berlin Wall – the man's figure is scratched out. "The greatest risk is in not taking one. AIG world leaders in insurance and financial services."

5. Man seen holding sign at street corner: "Homeless and hungry."

6. Mom: "If all your friends jumped off a cliff, would you?
   Joey: "Yes, where's the cliff?"

7. "Join millions of Americans in the Freedom Club."

8. Bert: "I heard that Greenland is applying to become the 51st state in the Union."
   Clyde: "I heard that also. Maybe it's true."

9. "Most Americans support the Equal Rights Amendment."

10. "I've just invented a perpetual motion machine which can run your car, power your house, and solve marital disputes, all at once by just adding water. Unfortunately the government is attempting to cover my discovery up because Exxon and Mobil would lose too much money, and now nobody believes me. Just send me $982 plus your firstborn son and you can have one."

Lesson 31

Exigency

An exigency is an urgent need which demands immediate action. The *exigency* technique encourages us to "hurry up and agree, because we are running out of time."

EXAMPLE A

"Genuine lead teacups! Now 95% off! Hurry, while supplies last!"

This advertisement is motivating us to make up our minds and do what the speaker says before all the lead teacups are gone. They want us to buy them so quickly that we don't think about whether we really need lead teacups.

Exigency **is being used when nothing more than a time limit is given as a reason for you to do what someone wants.**

EXAMPLE B

Caleb: "Why don't you come to that movie with me?"
Isaac: "I don't think I should. My parents haven't seen it yet, and we don't know if it is any good."
Caleb: "But it's been playing at the theaters for several weeks, and if we wait any longer, it might not be playing any longer."

In this example, Caleb isn't addressing the point which Isaac brought up (that his parents haven't seen it yet). Caleb is only talking about how the movie won't be playing for much longer.

Exercises

What form of propaganda, if any, is being used in the following exercises?

1. "Boy, these things have been selling like hotcakes. Better hurry up and get one before they are all gone."

2. "How much do you love your Camry? Camry is America's favorite car for the 4th year in a row, with more repeat buyers than any other car."

3. "Interest on a loan is at a really low rate right now – 1%. Last time it was this low it only stayed there for a few months, then it went up really high. I encourage you to get a loan for a new house."

4. "Discover why thousands of people with low vision have purchased the VideoEye."

5. Mr.: "Come on, why won't you marry me today?"
   Miss: "Oh, I can't make up my mind. I only met you this morning. Don't you think it's a little early?"
   Mr.: "I'm leaving tonight and won't be back for several years. If you don't marry me now, we may never get another chance."

6. "Donate blood today. Due to the recent disaster, thousands are in immediate need of your giving."

7. "Time is running out for you to take advantage of the Carpet Country carpet sale!"

8. "Since these genuine silver spoon sets are intended to be collector's items, they will only be available for a short time."

9. An advertisement for a arthritis pain relief drug features a picture of an elderly lady exercising in a park. Caption reads: "The #1 prescription arthritis medicine."

10. "Quick, Pa! The cows are loose and they're eatin' the neighbor's corn."

11. Kid, attempting to get you to sign up for the paper: "I've been delivering this paper to your neighbors on both sides for two years."

12. "I'm only going to be in town for a short time, so if you want one, you need to make up your mind soon."

13. "The price of stock in our company has been rising rapidly over the past few weeks, but this won't go on forever; sooner or later the price is going to peak and then drop. You need to buy soon before it reaches its peak."

Lesson 32

Repetition

A dolf Hitler once said "if you can tell a lie long enough and hard enough, sooner or later, people will start believing it." (Or maybe it was someone else who said that.)

Repetition **is repeating a message loudly and very often in the hope that it will soon be believed.**

EXAMPLE A

"Eat Sugarloops for breakfast! Eat Sugarloops for lunch! Eat Sugarloops for supper! Eat Sugarloops all the time! You will love Sugarloops."

Here, the technique is to drive the thought of eating Sugarloops into our heads – whether or not we would like to eat them at first. The advertiser hopes we will fall under his hypnotic spell and uncontrollably walk over to the cereal aisle of the supermarket mumbling "eat Sugarloops...must eat Sugarloops...."

Unlike the example above, sometimes this form of propaganda can't be noticed from only a single quotation. Repetition is also being used when we are bombarded constantly with lies. The liar thinks that if he tells the lie often, and the truth is not heard, then people will believe his lie.

Some scientists use this method when they want people to believe in their shaky theories. If they constantly put their theory into textbooks, lectures, magazines, and National Geographic specials, then we hear only their theory and nothing else. They figure, sooner or later, people will believe it. Unfortunately, they are right. This is why it is very important to speak up for the truth, even if nobody else does. If people do not hear the truth, then they will be overcome by lies.

EXAMPLE B

"[Former U.S. President, Bill] Clinton…said that some have attempted to minimize the role of firearms in tragedies such as the murders…of seven people in a church in Fort Worth, Texas…

'Of course something horrible happened to that man's heart when he walked into that church in Texas. But we cannot use that as an excuse,' Clinton said.

He asserted that the solution is a sharing of responsibility and a refusal to duck facts, not a search for scapegoats or an attempt to blame all gun murders simply on human evil." – on the MSNBC website

Clinton knows that human evil is the only cause for human evil. But Bill Clinton also knows that if he says that guns cause us to commit crimes, and if he says it often enough, with no one correcting him, then people will likely believe him.

CALVIN AND HOBBES © Watterson. Reprinted with permission of UNIVERSAL PRESS SYNDICATE. All rights reserved.

Calvin uses repetition.

Exercises

A. 1. Name some lies which are told very often.

B. What form of propaganda, if any, is being used in the following exercises?

2. "Try the NEW ABSOLUTELY FREE Car-o-Matic car washer for thirty days. ABSOLUTELY FREE! This item is NEW! If you are not happy with the Car-O-Matic after thirty FREE days, then return it ABSOLUTELY FREE of charge."

3. "No blur. No distortion. No UFO's. Kodak Film. Share moments. Share life."

4. An advertisement for allergy medicine features a picture of man with a gas mask on. Caption reads: "Before nasal allergies change your life, make an easier change. All it takes is Flonase."

5. Picture of young child sucking her thumb. "Cancer patients aren't the only victims of this disease."

6. "You know what? You are nothing but a stinking bum. You do no work all day, and you sit around doing nothing. I can't believe how lazy you are. You are so lazy you are going to end up on welfare."

7. "Boy, it seems like everybody's buying one of those balloon gizmos. It must be the latest thing. I think I'll get one."

8. Clyde: "My mom's car can reach very high speeds."
Bert: "How do you know that?"
Clyde: "That's what my mom says, but I don't know how she would know."

9. "Free bagging. Free checking. Free sitting. Free buying. Everything's free at Northpark Mall."

10. Mom: "You're not going to wear *that* are you?"
Daughter: "Aw, mom. You're so old-fashioned. Everybody's wearing these nowadays."

11. "For ten years I have been telling people that aliens have landed on earth. Finally, people are beginning to believe me!"

12. Letter to publisher: "I am writing to complain about the recent refusal of my book manuscript, *The Fallacy Detective*. I don't think your refusal to publish my book is right. That particular book took me over 5 years of solid work, without a day of rest. I worked on it so much that the letters on my keyboard are all worn off. I put my whole life into this book, and all you send me is a Post-It note saying: 'We are not considering publishing a book on logic at this time.' I was heartbroken. It has caused me to lose my sanity. I am now a raving maniac."

13. "Clean your house. Clean your car. Clean your garage. Make everything clean with Drakamine."

14. "Ford Explorer."

Lesson 33

Transfer

Transfer is a propaganda technique in which someone tries to make us transfer our good or bad feelings about one thing to another unrelated thing.

Commercials for cleaning products which feature images of spotlessly clean and bright clothes, houses with everything white, and good-looking people, are often examples of transfer. The advertiser wants us to transfer our feelings about clean houses and things to their product.

EXAMPLE A

In a commercial, a handsome man with big, bulging muscles is seen working out on the new "Gutwrencher" exercise machine. "Tone up your muscles in two weeks!" it says.

While this advertiser wouldn't actually say it, he wants us to transfer our feelings about the muscular man to the exercise machine. He wants us to think that if we would only buy the exercise machine, then our muscles will start to grow on their own, and, in a few weeks, we will end up looking like the muscular man.

Transfer can also be used to transfer negative feelings.

EXAMPLE B

Fuzzy images of Candidate B are shown in a television commercial. Candidate B is shown on a rainy day and he is wearing a mismatching suit. Discordant music is being played in the background. Next: a clean image of Candidate A is shown on a clear day in a clean and neat suit. A band is playing marching music. A voice says: "Vote for Candidate A. He knows how to govern."

When people see unclear pictures and hear obnoxious music they start to feel uncomfortable. If the advertiser can make us feel uncomfortable whenever we think about Candidate B, then we will probably feel less inclined to vote for him. If, on the other hand, we see clean images of Candidate A, and we hear upbeat inspirational music at the same time, then we might feel more inclined to vote for him when we go to the voting booth.

Transfer is also used when a famous celebrity is used to promote a product.

EXAMPLE C

In a commercial, Gara Gorgeous, the famous movie star with beautiful hair, holds up a bottle of shampoo and says, "Use Shimmer Bounce shampoo for better-looking and -smelling hair."

The advertiser wants us to transfer our good feelings for the famous movie star to the shampoo. While Gara Gorgeous's hair was probably done by a professional just before the filming, the advertiser is hoping we will think that her hair is good-looking because she used Shimmer Bounce shampoo.

Transfer is also used in the naming of products.

EXAMPLE D

"Purefresh Mountain Spring Water"

The name of this product makes us feel like their water is somehow purer and healthier than the everyday kind. They might have gotten it out of the tap, just like everybody else.

Not Transfer

Transfer is not being used when the famous person promoting a product is actually an authority on products of that kind.

EXAMPLE E

Jack Wack, the famous baseball pitcher, is shown holding up a certain kind of baseball glove: "I always use Atlanta Socker gloves when I pitch. It is the best glove out there."

Jack Wack may have a good reason for using that particular kind of glove – that is, if he actually uses it. We have a reason to believe Atlanta Socker gloves are good.

Exercises

What form of propaganda, if any, is being used in the following exercises?

1. Jack Wack, the famous baseball pitcher, says on a commercial: "I always use Stink-A-Way deodorant when playing a game – it helps me to smell fresh."

2. Joe Blowe, the famous boxer, is seen on a TV commercial: "I always exercise with the Gutwrencher exercise machine. I think it helps to build my bulging muscles so I can be a better boxer."

3. "Ladies and gentlemen of the jury, I urge you to convict this man and send him to a place where he can't commit any crimes. If you don't, you may be his next victim."

4. A picture of a bottle of soda pop covered in ice. The caption reads: "Refreshing!"

5. Picture of man on top of very tall tower. He says: "Car insurance with no State Farm agent? Now that scares me."

6. "Chevy Blazer."

7. An advertisement for cat food shows a picture of a house cat next to a large cougar: "Inside your cat live a thousand generations of big cats. Cats with an insatiable craving for meat. With that in mind, our cat food is made with real chicken."

8. "Every time you choose to buy a leather jacket or leather shoes, you sentence an animal to a lifetime of suffering.... Fashion should be fun, not grisly!" – from the "People for the Ethical Treatment of Animals" website.

9. A sport utility vehicle advertisement features an imposing picture of an SUV perched on a rock. Mountains are in the background.

10. "Why can't we go to Disneyland? We probably won't be in California again for several years. This is our only chance."

11. Man at the door: "Hello. My name is Scott. I just stopped by to get your opinion on a new encyclopedia. It is very up-to-date and has many different features in it – things such as large sections on each country of the world, with up-to-date information on their geography and current events. In the back, it has poster-size perforated pages of each of the American presidents, with statistics on each. Only you know if you need this kind of book or have the money to buy it. I have a plan which you can use to pay for it over a period of a year. Like I said, it's up to you.... Boy, it sure is a hot day out today. I was just talking to your neighbors down the road.... Oh, you know them very well? ... Well, I was talking to them and they couldn't figure out whether they needed this, but after thinking about it, they decided it was important to them."

12. A happy scene of a father with young son. Caption reads: "I will blink and they will be grown. At least with my Blue Cross and Blue Shield Plan, I have the power to choose what's right, so I can take charge of their health until they can stand alone. Meanwhile, I will treasure each embrace. This my plan: to take care of their mind, their body, their spirit, their health."

13. "BFV Motors has now produced over a hundred million cars. A hundred million cars owned by a hundred million drivers."

14. "There's something to be said for the pristine rivers, the breathtaking vistas, the removable third-row seat. Chevy Tahoe. Like a rock."

Lesson 34

Snob Appeal

Snob appeal is the opposite of bandwagon. While Bandwagon appeals to our desire to be like everyone else, snob appeal uses our desire to stand out from the rest of the crowd.

Snob appeal **is used when someone tries to persuade us to think their product would make us better, or stand out, from everyone else.**

Nobody wants to think he is merely one person among a crowd. We all like to think we're in a small and special community of people – in the uppity -ups.

EXAMPLE A

Advertisement: "Why read those boring logic books like everybody else does? You know you're better than that. You need more intellectual stimulation. Read *The Fallacy Detective*, and be more logical than the rest."

Snob appeal uses a ridiculous, but very effective, line: "Agree with me and buy my product because hardly anybody else does." This is an appeal to our inner snob.

But stop and think for a minute. Maybe there is a good reason why nobody else is doing it.

EXAMPLE B

"Buy Skunk brand perfume. You will stand out from the crowd."

Military recruiting posters cater to those who want to be "the best of the best."

EXAMPLE C

"Marines. Do you have what it takes?"

Parents who want their children to be distinguished may fall into this trap as well.

EXAMPLE D

"Use the classical approach. You're better than the average homeschooler."

The fallacy of snob appeal exploits our desire to be raised up to a higher class. We think that if we purchase the item, then greater glamour and prestige will be given to us. We will become better than everybody else.

Exercises

What form of propaganda, if any, is being used?

1. "SPURKEY is a nutritious food. SPURKEY tastes good. Doctors everywhere recommend SPURKEY as a dietary supplement. Remember SPURKEY the next time you go to the grocery store. SPURKEY for America and America for SPURKEY."

2. Picture of an SUV driving on rocky terrain. "It's a rough world. Use the proper equipment."

3. "Envy is so much more pleasant when you're on the receiving end." – A Mitsubishi car advertisement.

4. "The Smiths are doing it."

5. "We shouldn't proceed with the trial of the President. The American people are tired, and want to get this over with. If you proceed with the trial, then you will be proceeding with something which the American people do not want."

6. "You don't own a common herd of beef or dairy cattle, so why consider planting a common rye grass pasture? Your cattle investment is best protected by planting Southern Star." – Agricultural brochure

7. A picture of a porcupine next to a bottle of orange juice. Caption reads: "Our premium orange juice helps support your natural defenses. It only takes a minute, but the feeling lasts all day."

8. "Hey, I hope you agree with us that squealing to the cops isn't the most sociable thing to do. I wouldn't want to lose my best safecracker."

9. "We admit it: *The Complete Homeschooler* magazine isn't for everyone. But it is for you if: (a) You would like your children someday to receive full-tuition scholarships to top colleges and not to be saddled with huge loans for second-rate degrees. (b) You care even more about their spiritual state, and want them to be ready to change the world, not to be changed by the world."

10. An eye-poppingly colorful picture of a frog. Caption reads: "Wildlife as Canon sees it."

11. "Join Michael Douglas, John Travolta, and Bruce Willis in owning one of these delightful miniatures." – A rather expensive toy catalogue.

12. Advertisement: Picture of a fancy and fast-looking sedan. "Millions of people are perfectly happy driving boring cars. What makes you so special?"

13. Nissan advertisement: "May promote feelings of superiority."

14. Picture of presidential limo. "On the first day in office, every U.S. president has four things in common with his predecessor. Transporting the Chief on the wings of Goodyear. Goodyear. Specially-designed tires for the leader of the free world."

15. "Florida: America's most popular vacation destination."

16. Defense attorney: "My client admits to committing this crime. However, he has cancer and has only a year to live. I think it would be cruel to make a man go to prison when he is in such great pain."

17. "Buy the Chet Atkins Signature Gibson Guitar."

18. "Are you a rising young executive? Our line of luxury hotels caters to people with a taste for the better things in life."

Lesson 35

Appeal to Tradition and Appeal to Hi-Tech

When someone makes an *appeal to tradition*, he encourages us to buy some product or to take some action because it is associated with things of the past.

This propaganda technique appeals to old-fashioned folk who like old-fashioned traditions.

EXAMPLE A

A black-and-white photograph of man building a guitar. The caption reads: "Play Martin Guitars. Our expert guitar craftsmen build guitars using only the most time-honored traditions."

Advertising slogans which mention the age of the business are using tradition. "Established in 1919." "We've been in business for over 100 years." They want you to buy because they've been around for a long time. Their age may actually have little to do with their present service.

EXAMPLE B

A black-and-white photograph of an old 1950s coupe on one page, and on the next a picture of a smart, modern-looking coupe whizzing down the road. Caption reads: "Ford Thunderbird: yesterday, today, and tomorrow."

The first part of this advertisement is an appeal to tradition. It appeals to the sense of stability we get from owning something which has been around for a long time. The second part of the advertisement uses the propaganda technique called *appeal to hi-tech*.

In an *appeal to hi-tech*, we are encouraged to buy something because it is the "latest thing" – not necessarily because it is the best thing.

The picture of the up-to-date car appeals to the good feelings which we may have when we own something which is very new and up-to-date.

EXAMPLE C

Clyde: "Hey, Bert, you need to buy a pair of these new Niko shoes. They have hi-tech Dinotraction. It's a new special feature which helps you cling onto the back of a running plesiosaur without falling off."

This may be hi-tech, but do I need it? The hi-tech technique is also used when someone uses nonunderstandable technical terms to make his product seem very sophisticated.

EXAMPLE D

"Our Laundry Ball cleans your clothes automatically with our patented method of defusing the ionization of the fetezoic acids and implanting a catalyst."

Nobody knows what these terms mean, but they sure sound impressive.

Sometimes people use big words to make themselves sound impressive.

Exercises

What form of propaganda, if any, is being used?

1. President: "We need to pass this Nuclear Test Ban Treaty. At any moment, this world could be propelled into a nuclear holocaust."

2. Picture of George Washington holding a camcorder: "Where the old meets the new. Washington, D.C."

3. "Explosive effects. Dynamic dialogue. Pointed plot. Charismatic characters. This movie is for you."

4. Picture of a car being driven in the rain, precariously. Caption: "Treacherous. Could you regain control? Count on Shell."

5. "In order to unlock the secrets of the ocean, Dr. Robert Ballard uses the most sophisticated underwater equipment – including his Rolex Submariner watch."

6. Picture of an old Chevy Suburban next to picture of new Chevy Suburban: "Established 1935. Reestablished every year since."

7. "Experience the remarkable attraction of Jenn-Air ovens. For decades, we've been perfecting downdraft ventilation to beautifully clear the air without an overhead hood."

8. "We've been travelin' for several days now, and it seems as if every time we go into a grocery store, gas station, or restaurant, they're playin' country music. I think we're in Texas."

9. "Do you feel as if you are not at your best? Do you feel weak and tired all of the time? Maybe it's because you have parasites living inside you. Parasites are little bugs which live inside you and sap energy from your body. Doctors are beginning to realize that parasites are a leading cause of ill-feeling. Our new patented formula, called 'Bug Away,' helps to remove harmful parasites from your body."

10. "For happier smiles, happier faces, happier families, happier communities, and a happier world. State Ranch Life Insurance."

11. "Café de Columbia coffee. Aroma therapy since 1960."

12. "Visit historic Fredricksport for a touch of the past."

13. "Picked by over one million auto owners as the best sport utility vehicle."

14. Magazine advertisement with a picture of a small, malnourished, child. Caption: "Doesn't this poor African child deserve your help?"

15. "Stink-A-Way air freshener. Now with D-432 added for comfort."

16. "But Dad, this will be my last chance to buy that new dress before they run out."

17. A magazine advertisement for Old Country Root Beer features a black-and-white picture of some people rolling a barrel of Old Country Root Beer onto an old pickup truck. Caption reads: "Some things never change."

18. "The Colorado Balrog Bush is dying out. We need to halt all logging in the western states until we deal with this problem."

Lesson 36

Find Some Propaganda on Your Own

Exercises

A. The following examples of propaganda use methods not covered in this book. Identify the emotion being appealed to in each.

1. Picture of a young man in uniform next to his devoted parents: "He's not only my son. He's my hero. Today's Military. Proud parents. Bright futures."

2. Picture of a prairie chicken pecking at some grass: "The Greater Prairie Chicken is one of several species to benefit from the latest conservation effort by Phillips Petroleum. Together with the National Fish and Wildlife Foundation, Phillips will help restore and manage 19,500 acres of northwestern Missouri, making it a safe haven for high-priority birds. It's just one more way Phillips works to improve our world and why we're known as the Performance Company. Phillips Petroleum Company."

3. "I've just invented a perpetual motion machine which can run your car, power your house, and solve marital disputes all at one time, just by adding water. Unfortunately, the government wants to cover up my discovery because Exxon and Mobil would lose billions, so now nobody believes me. Just send me $982 plus your firstborn son and you can have one of my perpetual motion machines."

4. "Oh, a band'll do it, my friends, oh, yes! I mean a Boy's Band. Do
you hear me? I say River City's gotta have a Boy's Band, and I
mean she needs it today. Well, Professor Harold Hill's on hand,
River City's gonna have her Boy's Band! And just as the Lord
made little green apples, and that band's gonna be in uniform!
Johnny, Willy, Teddy, Fred! And you'll see the glitter of crashing
cymbals. And you'll hear the thunder of rolling drums and the
shimmer of trumpets. Tah-ta-ra and you'll feel something akin
to the electric thrill I once enjoyed when Gilmore, Liberatti, Pat
Conway, The Great Creatore, W. C. Handy, and John Philip
Sousa all came to town on the very same historic day!" – Professor
Harold Hill in *The Music Man*

B. 5. Take a current magazine – like *National Geographic*, *Time*, or *Reader's
Digest* – and look through all the advertisements in it. Find as many propaganda techniques as you can in the advertisements. You could do the
same thing with television commercials.

7

The Fallacy
Detective Game

Game Rules

Inventors' Note

This game was invented by Nathaniel and Hans Bluedorn, with some help from family members and friends. This game is more about making up your own examples of logical fallacies and propaganda techniques than it is learning how to recognize logical fallacies and propaganda techniques. We find that doing the former is much more fun.

We hope this game will be enjoyable for all kinds of people. If you have any improvements on it, or if you have a different idea for a logical fallacy game, please send us your ideas.

Preparation

1. Though three players can play this game, it is best played by four or more players. Each player must know what a fallacy is, and what a propaganda technique is. (You may refer players to the sections of this book which explain fallacies and propaganda techniques.)
   Hint: All of the fallacies covered in this book, with definitions and examples, are listed at the end of this section. You might want to make copies of this list to give to each player.
2. Each player must have paper and a pen or pencil.
3. The players must decide whether they will allow all fallacies in this book as examples, or whether they will limit the game to the fallacies in one section.
   Hint: For beginning players, we recommend that the game be

limited to the propaganda techniques in the propaganda section of this book. We think propaganda examples are easier to write and more enjoyable to play with.

Example Game: Players decide to use only *Section Six, Propaganda*, in this game.

Playing the Game

1. All players must create an example of a fallacy or propaganda technique, and write it down – allowing no one else to see what they wrote. Beside their example, they must also write the name of the fallacy or propaganda technique which they have used in their example.
   Hint: Creating examples will become easier with each round of the game.

   Example Game: Players Bert, Clyde, Jenny, and Sylvia each write down their examples according to the section they picked – Propaganda. Bert writes on paper the following example: "A picture of a fur-coat-clad mother hugging young son. Caption reads: 'Feel all warm and fuzzy with our insurance plan.'" Bert also writes what propaganda technique he thinks this is: "Transfer."

2. One person is chosen to be the first Reader. This person reads the examples from each player, including his own example. He does not say who wrote each example, or what he thinks the names of the fallacies are.

   Example Game: Jenny is elected as the Reader. She reads the examples from all the players.

3. Each player secretly writes down which example they think was the best. "Best" means whatever each person wants it to mean – funniest, most convincing, or whatever. A player may vote for his own example. The Reader also votes for an example. Each player must *write* his vote down – he cannot *say aloud* which example he is voting for.

4. Each player secretly writes down the name or description of the type of logical fallacy which he has voted for. He may refer to the chart if he likes.

5. After everyone has finished writing down their votes, then, beginning with the player to the left of the Reader, each player now reads aloud the fallacy he voted for and the name or description of that fallacy.

Example Game: Clyde voted for what happened to be Bert's example, and said it was transfer. Jenny voted for Clyde's example, and said it was exigency. Sylvia also voted for Bert's example, and said it was snob appeal. Bert voted for Sylvia's example, and said it was an appeal to fear. Of course, nobody knew who wrote the example he voted for.

6. The Reader counts the votes, and determines which example received the most votes for being "best." If the vote count is tied, then revote. If the vote count is tied again, then revote again.

Example Game: Bert's example is in the majority and is declared the "best."

7. The Reader then determines if the majority votes all agree as to the name of the fallacy they voted for. If some of them disagree, then the Reader determines which fallacy name is in the majority. This fallacy name is assumed to be the correct fallacy in the example. The player who wrote the winning example may have incorrectly named his own example. This does not matter. The majority rules in this game. However, if there is a tie, the person who wrote the example determines what fallacy it is.

Example Game: Since both Clyde and Sylvia voted for Bert's example, his fallacy is declared the "best." But there is a tie. Clyde thinks Bert's example is transfer, while Sylvia thinks Bert's example is snob appeal. Since Bert called it transfer when he created it, what he said is declared the "correct" answer.

Points

1. The player who wrote the best example receives two points.

2. Each player who voted for the best example receives one point.

3. Each player who voted for the best example, and who correctly named or described the fallacy or propaganda technique (was in the majority) receives one additional point. Only the Reader does *not* receive a point for guessing correctly the name of the fallacy or propaganda technique he voted for.

4. Points are added up and kept on a separate paper.

5. Note: If the player who wrote the winning fallacy also voted for his own fallacy, then he receives three points. And if he correctly named his own fallacy, he receives four points.

Example Game: Bert receives two points because his fallacy was the "best." Sylvia receives one point because she voted for Bert's example, but she did not correctly guess the fallacy name. Clyde receives two points because he voted for Bert's example and correctly guessed the fallacy. Jenny receives no points because she missed all of the above.

Continued Play

1. Play continues with each player writing another fallacy. The next Reader is the player to the right of the previous Reader.

2. The game ends after everyone has had a chance to be the Reader. Or, at the beginning of the game, players may agree to end the game when one player reaches a certain number of points.

Avoiding the Question

1. *Red Herring*: Introducing an irrelevant point into an argument. Someone may think (or may want *us* to think) it proves his side, but it really doesn't.
   - Grizzly bears can't be dangerous – they look so cute.
   - When the presidential candidate was asked whether he'd name as a running mate someone who was opposed to abortion, he replied: "It would be incredibly presumptive for someone who has yet to earn his party's nomination to be picking a vice president. However, the main criterion I would use in choosing a running mate would be whether the person was capable of being president."

2. *Ad Hominem*: Attacking an opponent's character, or his motives for believing something, instead of disproving his argument.
   - Jenny: "My uncle says that all murderers should be put to death because then nobody would want to murder anybody anymore." Sylvia: "Wasn't your uncle in jail once? I don't think that we can trust somebody's opinion who was once a criminal."
   - I know everybody thinks Einstein's theory of relativity is correct, but I can't accept it. Einstein believed in evolution.

3. *Genetic Fallacy*: Condemning an argument because of where it began, how it began, or who began it.
   - Jenny: "I think abortion is the murder of innocent children." Clyde: "The only reason why you disagree with abortion is because you were abused as a child and you have never recovered from it."
   - Bert: "Mr. Gritchus, why do you always wear suspenders and never a belt?" Mr. Gritchus: "Because belts were developed in the military centuries ago and were used by soldiers. Since the military is evil, and belts came from the military, therefore I can't wear a belt."

4. *Tu Quoque (You Too)*: Dismissing someone's viewpoint on an issue because he himself is inconsistent in that very thing.
   - Fred: "I wouldn't smoke cigarettes if I were you. It is a bad habit and it will bring you all kinds of problems." Jake: "Don't tell me not to smoke. You do it, too."
   - I don't see what is wrong with speeding – everybody does it.

5. *Faulty Appeal to Authority*: Appealing to the authority of someone who has no special knowledge in the area they are discussing.
   - My car mechanic says the best way to fix computer problems is to just give the computer a good, sharp kick.
   - Bert: "I've been homeschooled all of my life, and I think it has helped me out a lot." Clyde: "The man who has the highest IQ in the world said he didn't think homeschooling turned out good citizens. He said he didn't think homeschoolers received enough socialization, so they will become social misfits. Do you still think homeschooling is a good idea?"

6. *Appeal to the People*: Claiming that a viewpoint is correct just because many other people agree with it.
   - Political Candidate: "My opponent says abortion is murder – despite the fact that a recent poll concluded 76% of Americans believe an abortion does not murder an innocent child."
   - It looks as if more people vacation in Florida than any other place. It must be the nicest place in America to visit.

Making Assumptions

1. *Circular Reasoning*: Attempting to prove a conclusion by simply restating it. Someone says "P is true because Q is true, and Q is true because P is true."
   - Jimmy: "Dad, why do I have to learn logic?" Dad: "Because it will help to develop your mind." Jimmy: "Why will it develop my mind?" Dad: "Because it will help you think better."

2. *Equivocation*: Changing the meaning of a word in the middle of an argument.
   - If the English don't drive on the right side of the road, what are they doing on the wrong side?
   - Dad: "Son, when you grow up I want you to always be a responsible young man." Son: "But Dad, I am already very responsible. Whenever something breaks around here, it seems as if I am always responsible."

3. *Loaded Question*: Asking one question which assumes the answer to a second question.
   - Neighbor: "Why do you like to disturb the neighborhood by playing your music so loud everybody can hear it a mile away?" [Does the neighbor really like to disturb the neighborhood?]
   - Judge: "Have you stopped beating your poor dog yet?" [Has he ever begun beating his dog?]

4. *Part-to-Whole*: Asserting that what is true of part of something must also be true of the whole thing together.
   - Child: "Mommy, why is this feather pillow so heavy? It only has feathers in it, and little feathers weigh hardly anything."
   - If I can break this bunch of sticks, one by one, Mommy, why can't I break a bunch of sticks together?

5. *Whole-to-Part*: Asserting that what is true of something as a whole must also be true of each of its parts. This is the reverse of the part-to-whole fallacy.
   - If our bag of potato chips won't float when I throw it in the pond, why will one of my potato chips float by itself?
   - If I can't break this bunch of sticks, all at once, Mommy, shouldn't I be unable to break each individual stick?

6. *Either-Or*: Asserting that we must chose between two things, when in fact we have more alternatives.
   - Either you're an American or you are a Communist. You aren't from America, so you must be a Communist.
   - Either you believe in evolution, or you are totally irrational. You say you don't believe in evolution, so you must be irrational.

Statistical Fallacies

1. *Hasty Generalization*: Generalizing about a class or group based upon a small and poor sample.
   - All plumbers are brilliant. I know a plumber who can calculate the value of pi to the 289,954th digit.
   - Southerners talk fast. I was just on the phone with one and he sure talked fast.

2. *Weak Analogy*: Claiming that some items which have only a few minor similarities are practically the same in almost everything else.
   - Clyde: "I think it is all right for governments in developing countries to execute citizens who don't agree with the government. If you want to make an omelet, then you have to break a few eggs."
   - A cloud is 75% water. A watermelon is 75% water. Since a plane can fly through a cloud, therefore a plane can fly through a watermelon.

3. *Post hoc ergo propter hoc*: Assuming that since A happened before B, A must have caused B.
   - Our rooster crows every morning. Then the sun comes up. Now do you understand how important roosters are?
   - Christianity came along in the first century, and a few hundred years after that, the Roman Empire fell. Christianity must have made it fall.

4. *Proof by lack of evidence*: Claiming something is true simply because nobody has yet given any evidence to the contrary.
   - There must be mountain lions living in Illinois, because I haven't seen any proof that none exist.
   - No evidence has been found that life does not exist on other planets. Therefore, we are not alone in the universe.

Propaganda

1. *Appeal to Fear*: Moving you to fear the consequences of not doing what he wants.
   - Prosecuting Attorney: "Ladies and gentlemen of the jury, I urge you to convict John Jones of this crime of murder. We need to put him where he can never commit any crimes. If you don't convict him, you may be his next victim."
   - Restaurant owner: "You no lika da pizzas? I send over my cousin Tony for a little change a' mind. He maka you lika da pizzas."
   - Do you know what kind of damage a loose cow can do on your farm? Imagine what would happen if your electric fence failed and your cows wandered into the neighbors field. Buy a "Zapper" electric fence and you won't have to worry about it.

2. *Appeal to Pity*: Urging someone to do something only because they pity us, or they pity something associated with us.
   - Radio advertisement: "Mr. Jones lost the last election because his opponent used a smear campaign to discredit him. Mr. Jones lost the election before that because of voter fraud. Don't you think it is about time you voted for Mr. Jones?"
   - Motorist: "But, officer, this is the fifth ticket I've been given this year. If I get another ticket, then they will take my license away, and I won't be able to drive to work. My wife and children will starve."

3. *Bandwagon*: Pressuring someone to do something just because many other people are doing it.
   - Clyde: "Dad, can I go to see the movie 'Attack of the Killer Wombats'?" Dad: "No, son, you can't go. I heard that movie has bad things in it." Clyde: "Aw, come on, everybody's going to see it."
   - "More Americans get their news from ABC than from any other source."

4. *Exigency*: Offering nothing more than a time limit as a reason for us to do what someone wants.

- Genuine lead teacups! Now 95% off! Hurry, while supplies last!
- Mr.: "Come on, why don't you marry me today?" Miss: "Oh, I can't make up my mind. I only met you this morning. Don't you think it is a little early?" Mr.: "I'm leaving tonight and won't be back for several years. If you don't marry me now, we may never have another chance."

5. *Repetition*: Repeating a message loudly and very often in the hope that it will eventually be believed.
- Eat Sugarloops for breakfast! Eat Sugarloops for lunch! Eat Sugarloops for supper! Eat Sugarloops all the time! You will love Sugarloops.

6. *Transfer*: Attempting to get someone to associate his good or bad feelings about one thing to another unrelated thing.
- In a commercial, a handsome man with big, bulging muscles is seen working out on the new "Gutwrencher" exercise machine. The announcer says,"Tone up your muscles in two weeks!"
- In a commercial, Gara Gorgeous, the famous movie star with beautiful hair, holds up a bottle of shampoo and says. "Use Shimmer Bounce shampoo for better-looking and better-smelling hair."
- "Purefresh Mountain Spring Water"

7. *Snob Appeal*: Encouraging someone to think that our product would make them better than or stand out from everybody else.
- Advertisement: "Why read those boring logic books like everybody else does? You know you're better than that. You need more intellectual stimulation. Read *The Fallacy Detective*. Be more logical than the rest."
- Buy skunk brand perfume. You will stand out in the crowd.

8. *Appeal to Tradition*: Encouraging someone to buy a product or do something because it is associated with something old.
- A black-and-white photograph of man building a guitar. The caption reads: "Play Martin Guitars. Our expert guitar craftsmen build guitars using only the most time-honored traditions."
- A black-and-white photograph of an old 1950s

coupe on one page, and on the next a picture of a smart, modern-looking coupe whizzing down the road. Caption reads: "Ford Thunderbird: yesterday, today, and tomorrow."

9. *Appeal to Hi-tech*: Urging someone to buy something because it is the "latest thing" – but not necessarily because it is the best thing.
- Clyde: "Hey, Bert, you need to buy one of these new Niko shoes. They have hi-tech 'Dinotraction.' It's a new special feature that helps you cling onto the back of a running plesiosaur without falling off."
- Our "Laundry Ball" cleans your clothes automatically with our patented method of defusing the ionization of the fetezoic acids and implanting a catalyst.

8

Answer Key

Answers

Lesson 1: Exercise Your Mind

1. a. Surfing should not be the only thing in life. Like, man, don't you agree?
2. a. Children have the amazing ability to forget things when it suits them. So do adults.
3. c. Ted isn't being lazy with his mind, but he might be lazy with his body.
4. a. Bradley's grandpa is probably trying to get his grandson to think about community issues.
5. b. Merle is making the effort to understand issues better.
6. Nathaniel: c. Blaine has a point. People with allergies shouldn't have to mow the lawn. Hans: a. Blaine is just trying to get out of working.
7. b. Newt is probably just complaining. He knows he likes to learn things.
8. c.

Lesson 2: Love to Listen

1. b. Gary doesn't like to listen. He doesn't want to hear people give their side of the issue.
2. Can't decide. Betty might just be tired.
3. b. Byron doesn't like to listen. He just made Webster listen for half an hour, but he will only listen to Webster for a few seconds.
4. c. Doesn't love to listen to loud music, which is understandable.
5. Depends. Generally it's good to listen to criticisms people have for you. But sometimes it can be too much.
6. b. It doesn't sound like Jim is actually worried that Nat is controlling

his life. He sounds more like he doesn't want to hear other people criticize his decisions.

7. a. Patty might think she talks too much, but she genuinely wants to listen more.

Lesson 3: Opposing Viewpoints

1. Example: the view of the Union, and the view of the Confederacy.
2. King George in England's view, and the views of the American Colonists.
3. Pro-abortion, and anti-abortion.
4. Christians, and atheists.
5. Homeschooling is bad for children, and homeschooling is good for children.
6. Golden Retriever vs. German Shepherd – obviously!
7. Gun control advocates, and Second Amendment rights advocates.
8. Creationists, and Evolutionists
9. Slaveholders in the South, and abolitionists in the North.
10. Those who read *The Fallacy Detective*, and those who don't read *The Fallacy Detective*.
11. The views of mothers, and the views of little boys.
12. Cubs vs. White Sox – obviously!

Lesson 4: Red Herring Fallacy

1. He is answering the question.
2. RED HERRING!
3. He is answering the question.
4. RED HERRING!
5. RED HERRING!
6. He is answering the question.
7. He is answering the question.
8. RED HERRING!

Lesson 5: Recognizing Red Herrings

1. Are grizzly bears dangerous? RED HERRING!
2. Should I study math? RED HERRING! This is not the point.
3. Should people read a book a month? The speaker addresses the topic.
4. Should the government raise taxes? The speaker addresses the topic.
5. Should the government lower taxes? RED HERRING! This shows the government is spending too much money on welfare. It does not show why we should lower taxes. We could eliminate welfare and spend the money somewhere else.
6. Should you believe in life after death? RED HERRING!
7. Would you name as a running mate someone who is pro-life? RED HERRING!
8. Did you ever take drugs? The speaker addresses the topic.
9. Did you cheat in school? Hans: I don't think this is a red herring. He doesn't try to avoid the question.
10. Should the federal government help schools? RED HERRING!
11. Is deforestation bad? RED HERRING!

Lesson 6: *Ad Hominem* Attack

1. *Ad hominem.*
2. None.
3. *Ad hominem.*
4. *Ad hominem.*
5. None.
6. *Ad hominem.*
7. Red herring.
8. *Ad hominem.*
9. *Ad hominem.*
10. Red herring.
11. None.
12. *Ad hominem.*

Lesson 7: Genetic Fallacy

1. None. This is probably true.
2. Genetic fallacy.
3. Genetic fallacy.
4. Red herring.
5. Red herring.
6. Genetic fallacy.
7. Genetic fallacy.
8. *Ad hominem.*
9. None. This is just stating a belief about the origins of fashion.
10. *Ad hominem.*

Lesson 8: *Tu Quoque*

1. *Tu quoque.*
2. *Ad hominem.*
3. Genetic fallacy.
4. None.
5. Red herring.
6. *Ad hominem.*
7. *Tu quoque.*
8. Red herring.
9. Red herring. They aren't arguing anymore over whether war is wrong in all cases.
10. *Tu quoque.*
11. None. This is merely his opinion.

Lesson 9: Faulty Appeal to Authority

1. Faulty appeal to authority. This man is not an authority on what happened at the scene of the crime.
2. Faulty appeal to authority.
3. Good appeal to authority.
4. Faulty appeal to authority.

5. Good appeal to authority. The violin teacher knows the topic.
6. Faulty appeal to authority.
7. Good appeal to authority.
8. Good appeal to authority.
9. None. Elizabeth Taylor is probably an expert on the subject of cosmetic surgery.
10. Red herring. He is changing the subject. They aren't arguing about why he took action. They are arguing about the kind of action he took.
11. Faulty appeal to authority.
12. None.
13. *Ad hominem.*

Lesson 10: Appeal to the People

1. Appeal to the people.
2. Faulty appeal to authority. This is a controversial topic.
3. Appeal to the people.
4. None.
5. *Tu quoque.*
6. Faulty appeal to authority. This is a very controversial subject.
7. Red herring. It does not say why corn growers need subsidies.
8. Appeal to the people.
9. Appeal to the people.
10. None. If the song is on the top of the charts it means many people are listening to it, which means it is popular.

Lesson 11: Straw Man

1. Straw man.
2. None. If the book is on the best-seller list, it must be popular.
3. Appeal to the people. Millions of Americans are not authorities on the subject of climate – we need to ask some people who know what they are talking about, and even then we need to examine many different viewpoints about a controversial subject.
4. Straw man.

5. Appeal to the people.
6. Red herring. The question is whether it is morally right to execute insane people, not whether banning the execution of insane people is a good idea.
7. Straw man.
8. Appeal to the people.
9. Genetic fallacy.
10. Straw man.
11. Faulty appeal to authority.
12. *Tu quoque.*

Lesson 12: The Story of Aroup Goupta

1. a. The story used the masculine pronoun for Aroup.
2. a. Yes, the story said he was in a city.
3. a. The story said he was in a capital city.
4. b. Gotcha. The story mentioned the country called Clovnia, but it did not say if that was where Aroup was.
5. a. It said so.
6. b. The story did not say what Aroup was doing.
7. a. It said so.
8. b. The story never mentioned his age.
9. a. He said that he was Aroup's friend, and we are supposed to believe everything the characters say.
10. a. The story said that it was a restaurant.
11. a. The story said it must have been Cloveneeze.
12. a. You can deduce from the story that he was a native Clovnian.
13. a. He could have been an FBI agent for all we know, but of course he could have worked at the restaurant.
14. a. It said so.
15. a. He said that was what he wanted.
16. b. The story never said who they were, or why they left the restaurant.
17. a. He said it tasted terrible.
18. a. The story said he felt the oatmeal in his tummy.
19. b. The age limit for drinking beet juice was never mentioned.

20. b. She never said she did.
21. b. The story didn't say that Aroup was in trouble.
22. b. The story did end.

Lesson 13: Assumptions

1. Yes.
2. Probably.
3. No. He said his Mom wants to buy an expensive toaster, but he didn't assume all toasters are expensive.
4. Yes. At least the type of ice cream Brent wants.
5. Yes.
6. No. This didn't even enter his mind.
7. One. If they sweep them together then they will have only one pile.
8. The first are worth $19.96 and the second are worth $19.67.
9. If you answered that cows drink milk, then you are wrong. Cows drink water, not milk. A cow would get sick if it drank milk. Notice how we got you to assume something obviously false by subtly suggesting it to your mind.

Lesson 14: Circular Reasoning

1. Circular reasoning.
2. Circular reasoning. You can trust him because he says he has never lied? What if he is lying when he says he is not lying?
3. Not circular reasoning.
4. Circular reasoning.
5. Circular reasoning.
6. Not circular reasoning.
7. Circular reasoning.
8. Not circular reasoning. The husband just has a selfish attitude.
9. Not circular reasoning. This is a fallacy which we haven't explained yet.
10. Circular reasoning.
11. Circular reasoning.
12. Faulty appeal to authority.
13. Genetic fallacy.

14. Faulty appeal to authority. Gun control is a controversial subject.
15. Yes. Real doctors are those who don't recommend echinacea, and we can know a doctor is real if he doesn't recommend echinacea.

Lesson 15: Equivocation

1. Equivocation on the word "pen."
2. Equivocation on the word "responsible."
3. Equivocation. The founding fathers meant by "equal," "equal under the law," not equal in abilities and incomes.
4. Equivocation on the word "intelligent."
5. None.
6. Equivocation on the word "uses."
7. Circular reasoning.
8. Equivocation on the word "cold."
9. None.
10. None.
11. Equivocation on the word "illegal."
12. Faulty appeal to authority.
13. Circular reasoning.
14. Equivocation on the word "Nobody."
15. None.
16. None yet.

Lesson 16: Loaded Question

1. Loaded question. Do you know the music you play can be heard a long distance away? Do you like to disturb the neighborhood?
2. Loaded question. Are you going to buy the Ford Bubblebox model car? If so, when?
3. None. A mother has the right to ask whatever questions she wants.
4. Loaded question "Will the state tourism bureau list our city as smelling bad if we don't ban leaf burning?" and "Should residents be allowed to burn leaves in front of city hall?" These controversial questions need to be answered first.

5. Huh? Probably a loaded question, but just because it is a question and looks suspicious.
6. Probably a loaded question. Is your business in danger of being broken into?
7. Did God make bathtubs?
8. Loaded question. The salesman assumes the lady wants to buy his products.
9. None.
10. Appeal to the people.
11. Circular reasoning.
12. Probably red herring.
13. Equivocation on the word "man."
14. None. Could be true.

Lesson 17: Part-to-Whole

1. Part-to-whole.
2. Part-to-whole.
3. Part-to-whole.
4. Not part-to-whole. We just added those "part … whole" words to confuse you.
5. Part-to-whole. If the parts of the universe are spherical, then the universe as a whole is spherical.
6. Part-to-whole. If all the parts of the human body were made for a function, then human beings as a whole also have a purpose.
7. Not part-to-whole.
8. Part-to-whole. The quality of the materials does not imply that the house was well constructed.
9. Part-to-whole. The facts that suits are well tailored does not imply that people who wear them will be distinguished and fashionable.
10. Not part-to-whole.
11. Part-to-whole. Just because you might find a mistake in our logic book, this doesn't mean that the whole subject of logic is false and shouldn't be studied.
12. Equivocation on the word "crime."
13. Loaded question. Is there evidence for mental telepathy?
14. Circular reasoning.

15. Red herring.
16. Faulty appeal to authority. Childrearing is a very controversial subject.

Lesson 18: Whole-to-Part

1. Whole-to-part. Not all of the parts of General Motors' cars are made by General Motors.
2. Whole-to-part. The Smith family as a whole may be a hardworking family, but Bubba Smith may not have those qualities by himself.
3. Whole-to-part. Even though the farm as a whole may be productive, any particular part of the farm may not be fertile.
4. Part-to-whole. If each individual is most efficient when he has personal liberty, then society as a whole will reach maximum efficiency if there is maximum personal liberty.
5. Whole-to-part. Just because the whole economy is booming does not mean that every sector – including the tweezers manufacturing sector – is booming.
6. None.
7. Part-to-whole. If each American is more aware of danger and is more careful, then all of American society will feel safer.
8. Whole-to-part. Just because you have a part of a magnificent structure in your home doesn't necessarily make your home any more magnificent.
9. Whole-to-part. Jim might be the only one on Team America who is a very bad athlete and didn't win any medals.
10. Whole-to-part. Harvard may have produced a few bad lawyers over the years.
11. None.
12. Whole-to-part. Just because the Reformation as a whole might have been a movement from God does not necessarily mean that every part of the Reformation was from God.
13. Loaded question.
14. Circular reasoning.
15. Equivocation on the word "reason."
16. Appeal to the people.
17. Faulty appeal to authority. The First Lady isn't necessarily an expert on this subject.

Lesson 19: Either-Or

1. Nathaniel: This is either-or. Hans: This is not either-or. It isn't either-or if there are truly only two choices. The farmer is making a good argument that there are only two choices in his experience. Make up your own mind.
2. Either-or.
3. Either-or.
4. Either-or. The Bandit forgot another possibility: "With a heroic bound, Zorro leapt out from the coach and caught the ruffian by the throat...."
5. Not either-or. A mother has the right to limit the alternatives.
6. Either-or.
7. Not either-or.
8. Not either-or.
9. Not either-or. What Dad says goes.
10. Either-or. The neighborhood children were having a huge squirt gun fight in the street. This is an either-or argument, even though the grumpy old lady considered more than two possibilities.
11. Either-or.
12. Either-or.
13. Circular reasoning.
14. Equivocation on the word "miracles."
15. Appeal to the people.
16. Faulty appeal to authority.
17. Part-to-whole. If it is wise for individuals to plan and control their lives, then is it wise for society as a whole to be planned and controlled?
18. Loaded question. Did someone take the fingernail clippers and hide them? If so, who was it?
19. Whole-to-part. All Americans don't share the general characteristics of the American way.
20. Neither. Cows don't drink milk. (Young calves do drink milk, but cows do not.) Notice how you were not aware of your assumptions when you answered that question? Be more alert next time.

Lesson 20: What Is a Generalization?

1. Generalization.
2. Generalization.
3. Generalization.
4. Not a generalization.
5. Generalization.
6. Not a generalization. There are parts of Alaska on the top of Mt. McKinley, so the statement is true.
7. Not a generalization. If the premises are true, the conclusion must also be true.
8. Generalization.
9. Generalization.
10. Generalization.
11. Not a generalization.
12. Generalization.
13. Not a generalization.
14. Generalization.
15. Answers will vary.

Lesson 21: Hasty Generalization

1. Generalization. Sample of one. Very hasty.
2. Generalization. Sample of 3,000. Hasty – probably only rich plumbers would have enough money to attend an international plumbers convention.
3. Generalization. Sample of one. Very hasty – she may teach you well, but there are many different kinds of learners in the world.
4. Not a generalization. "Some" means one or more. Since this man is brilliant (and we must assume he fits whatever he calls "brilliant"), he can accurately say some plumbers are brilliant.
5. Generalization. Sample of all of Dickens' novels. Probably not hasty – but his short stories or letters might be interesting.
6. Generalization. Sample: several times he took aspirin. Strong generalization.

7. Generalization. Sample of 5,000. If the barrel was mixed well, then it is a strong generalization.
8. Not a generalization. The data is complete.
9. Generalization. Sample of one. Very hasty.
10. This is not true. There have been many revolutions where no one was hurt or killed.
11. Answers will vary.
12. Answers will vary. It would be a good idea to study different breeds of pigs in different environments.
13. Answers will vary. You need to see many hairstylists.
14. Hans: I think this is strong. Nathaniel: I think this is weak. This would take a large sample of firstborns from all over the world.
15. Answers will vary. It would take a large sample of typists in general, and of one person's typing in particular, to decide whether this was a good generalization.
16. You need to survey people in all places of the world.
17. In our experience: true, except in Florida. It would take a large sample of people in all states south of the Mason-Dixon Line to decide whether this was a good generalization.
18. Answers will vary. A large sample of statistics may indicate this.
19. Probably strong – based on what we know of the communist governments we can think of.
20. Answers will vary.

Lesson 22: What Is an Analogy?

1. Analogy.
2. Generalization.
3. Generalization.
4. Analogy.
5. Analogy.
6. Neither.
7. Generalization.
8. Huh?
9. Neither.
10. Poetic analogy.
11. Poetic analogy.

12. Generalization.
13. Every time it rains the flowers will bloom
14. All southern states that are near the ocean will have palm trees.
15. You will never win a fight against anything that is big and mean, like Tony.

Lesson 23: Weak Analogy

1. Weakens.
2. Weakens.
3. Strengthens.
4. It might weaken.
5. Weakens.
6. Neither.
7. Strengthens.
8. Weakens.
9. Strengthens.
10. Weakens.
11. Weakens.
12. Interesting question...Hans: I really don't know.
13. Weakens – assuming you are not very young any longer.
14. Neither.
15. Neither.
16. Weakens.
17. Hans: I thought this was a strong analogy, but everybody seems to disagree with me. They all think this is weak. They say the location in the Midwest and near a large body of water has no apparent connection to crime problems.
18. Weak analogy.
19. Strong analogy.
20. Weak analogy. There is a great difference between one man's life and many, many generations of organisms.
21. Actually, there is much debate over this issue. Some people are afraid of saccharin because of this, and some think that is ridiculous. Hans: I say it is probably a weak analogy.
22. Probably strong.

23. Neither. This kind of poetic analogy isn't meant to be very scientific, but only to illustrate a point.
24. Neither. This kind of analogy isn't meant to be very scientific, but only to illustrate a point.
25. Weak analogy.
26. Lawyers and mosquitoes.
27. It doesn't really. There are some superficial similarities – such as general temperament.
28. That mosquitoes should be able to practice law (if they can pass the bar exam).
29. Answers will vary.
30. Chimpanzees and humans.
31. It doesn't really. It doesn't show how animals having some of the same genes and having some of the same social skills as humans makes them significantly similar to humans. It doesn't address the differences between humans and apes at all (such as the amount of hair, and the punch bowl).
32. That apes should have some of the same rights as humans.
33. Answers will vary. In our opinion, nothing compares with being made in the image of God.

Lesson 24: Post Hoc Ergo Propter Hoc

1. It is also possible that animosity between countries will cause them to build large armies, and if that animosity continues, there may be war.
2. It might be that I happen to wear those shoes whenever I am in a good mood, and whenever I am in a good mood, I do better on tests.
3. Circular reasoning.
4. *Post hoc ergo propter hoc.*
5. Whole-to-part. The power and resources of the United States government as a whole do not necessarily imply that the little mailman at the Wichiwachi Post Office is very powerful or resourceful.
6. Hasty generalization.
7. None.
8. Weak analogy.

9. *Post hoc ergo propter hoc.*
10. Either-or.
11. Weak analogy.
12. Straw man.
13. *Post hoc ergo propter hoc.*
14. Genetic fallacy.
15. *Post hoc ergo propter hoc.*
16. Faulty appeal to authority. Knowing Hebrew doesn't necessarily make you a better authority on baptism.
17. None.
18. Straw man.
19. Equivocation on the word "steal."

Lesson 25: Post Hoc Ergo Propter Hoc in Statistics

1. *Tu quoque.*
2. Either-or. He might have been running as an Independent.
3. *Post hoc ergo propter hoc.*
4. *Post hoc ergo propter hoc.*
5. None. This doesn't say one thing is causing the other.
6. *Post hoc ergo propter hoc.*
7. Circular reasoning.
8. None. This is not *post hoc ergo propter hoc* because another plausible reason is given for the increase in accidents.
9. None. This is a good appeal to authority.
10. *Post hoc ergo propter hoc.*
11. Hasty generalization. He may just become angry at the way you argue with him.
12. Loaded question.
13. *Post hoc ergo propter hoc.* The tattoo should be a signal to this father that he may have other things to worry about with his son.
14. *Post hoc ergo propter hoc.*
15. A gun in your home does not make you safer. You are more likely to use your gun to kill someone you know than to use it in self-defense.

16. It doesn't say. It could mean anything from a close family member to the guy down at the Seven-Eleven.

17. I don't think we could know. Guns are kept for many reasons, and it would be difficult to limit it to one reason.

18. They say that owning a gun is more likely to cause you, or one of your close friends, to shoot somebody you know.

19. A *New England Journal of Medicine* study that says a gun kept in the average home for self-protection is twenty-two times more likely to be used to kill someone the owner knows than to be used in self-defense.

20. How about this one: If you or your close friend is a criminal murderer, this is likely to cause one of you to go out and buy a gun to shoot somebody you know.

Lesson 26: Proof by Lack of Evidence

1. Prosecuting Attorney.
2. Proof by lack of evidence.
3. Weak analogy.
4. None.
5. Proof by lack of evidence.
6. Straw man.
7. Whole-to-part. Not all Frenchmen are sophisticated and artistic.
8. Weak analogy.
9. Proof by lack of evidence.
10. Either-or.
11. Either-or.
12. Genetic fallacy.
13. Proof by lack of evidence.
14. Equivocation on the word "fix."
15. *Post hoc ergo propter hoc.*
16. *Ad hominem.*
17. Appeal to the people.
18. *Post hoc ergo propter hoc.*
19. Proof by lack of evidence.
20. *Post hoc ergo propter hoc.*
21. *Post hoc ergo propter hoc.*
22. Proof by lack of evidence.

23. None.
24. *Post hoc ergo propter hoc.*
25. Proof by lack of evidence.
26. None. The researchers say nowhere that the cabbage is causing auto accidents.
27. Proof by lack of evidence.
28. Circular reasoning.
29. *Ad hominem.*

Lesson 27: What Is Propaganda?

1. All kinds: Advertisers, politicians, lawyers, your uncle…
2. No. Good people use propaganda. But, good people who are being good shouldn't use manipulative propaganda.
3. Advertisements, political speeches, in the courtroom, from your uncle.
4. No, propaganda is a general strategy for spreading our ideas. There is nothing wrong with spreading our ideas. But attempting to manipulate persons through their emotions is not good.
5. No. They can be correct. Swiss Springtime soap may be good soap, but that doesn't mean the manufacturer should manipulate our emotions.
6. No. When I tell you to that communism is wrong because it destroys society, I am not being manipulative, but I am propagating my beliefs, which is propaganda.
7. No. Propaganda doesn't have to be manipulative, but it often is.
8. No.
9. No.
10. Canberra.
11. Manipulative and emotional propaganda.
12. Manipulative and emotional propaganda.
13. Manipulative and emotional propaganda.
14. This is not manipulative and emotional propaganda. However, we would say it is impossible to prove that there is no God.
15. Manipulative and emotional propaganda.
16. Manipulative and emotional propaganda.

Lesson 28: Appeal to Fear

1. Appeal to fear – fear of a car accident.
2. Not an appeal to fear.
3. Appeal to fear – fear of the consequences if your cows get out.
4. Appeal to fear – fear of losing your job.
5. Appeal to fear – fear of losing school support.
6. This is a threat.
7. Appeal to fear – fear of corrupted kids.
8. This is an order.
9. This is a threat.
10. Appeal to fear – fear of lead poisoning.

Lesson 29: Appeal to Pity

1. Appeal to fear.
2. Appeal to pity. It doesn't say how controlling guns would solve the problem.
3. None – yet.
4. Appeal to pity. Teacher: "You should have thought about that when you were studying for the test."
5. Appeal to pity. He doesn't say that he actually needs any money.
6. None – assuming that he is telling the truth, the guy obviously needs help.
7. Appeal to fear – fear of losing the Kansas Board of Education.
8. Appeal to pity.
9. None – yet.
10. Appeal to pity.
11. None.
12. Appeal to both fear and pity.

Lesson 30: Bandwagon

1. Appeal to pity.
2. Bandwagon.

3. Bandwagon.
4. Appeal to fear.
5. Appeal to pity.
6. Bandwagon.
7. Bandwagon.
8. None.
9. Bandwagon.
10. None – yet.

Lesson 31: Exigency

1. Exigency. But, do I want one?
2. Bandwagon.
3. Exigency. What if I don't want a new house?
4. Bandwagon.
5. Exigency. He gives no real reason to marry him.
6. None. It gives a good reason to give blood today: many people need it.
7. Exigency.
8. Exigency.
9. Bandwagon.
10. None.
11. Bandwagon.
12. Exigency.
13. Exigency. But why should I invest in this company?

Lesson 32: Repetition

1. Answers will vary. Examples: The lie that we are not responsible for our actions. The lie that there is no God. The lie that abortion is only a "choice."
2. Repetition.
3. Repetition.
4. Appeal to fear. Exigency.
5. Appeal to pity and fear.
6. Repetition.
7. Bandwagon.

8. None.
9. Repetition.
10. Bandwagon.
11. Repetition.
12. Appeal to pity.
13. Repetition.
14. None – yet.

Lesson 33: Transfer

1. Transfer. Jack Wack has no special expertise in this subject.
2. None.
3. Appeal to fear – the fear of becoming a victim.
4. Transfer.
5. Appeal to fear.
6. Transfer. The title prompts us to think that the owner will automatically become a rugged individualist.
7. Transfer. Will our cat become a mountain lion if he eats their cat food?
8. Appeal to pity.
9. Transfer.
10. Exigency.
11. Bandwagon.
12. Transfer.
13. Bandwagon.
14. Transfer.

Lesson 34: Snob Appeal

1. Repetition.
2. Transfer.
3. Snob appeal.
4. Bandwagon.
5. Bandwagon.
6. Snob appeal.
7. Transfer.
8. Appeal to fear.

9. Snob appeal.

10. Transfer. They want you to think that if you owned a Canon camera, then you would be able to take pictures like the one shown.

11. Snob appeal.

12. Snob appeal.

13. Snob appeal.

14. Transfer and snob appeal.

15. Bandwagon.

16. Appeal to pity.

17. Snob appeal and transfer.

18. Snob appeal.

Lesson 35: Appeal to Tradition and Appeal to Hi-tech

1. Exigency and appeal to fear.

2. Transfer, tradition, and hi-tech.

3. Transfer and repetition.

4. Appeal to fear.

5. Hi-tech.

6. Tradition.

7. Tradition and Hi-tech.

8. None.

9. Appeal to fear and appeal to hi-tech.

10. Repetition.

11. Tradition.

12. Tradition.

13. Bandwagon.

14. Appeal to pity.

15. Hi-tech.

16. Exigency.

17. Tradition.

18. Exigency.

Lesson 36: Find Some Propaganda on Your Own

1. Patriotism and pride.
2. Phillips wants us to support their company because they care about the environment. We don't know if they make these efforts because they really care about the environment, or because they just want to be able to post advertisements like this.
3. This is the opposite of the bandwagon technique. If practically nobody in the world does a particular thing, then that thing must be good. These people think they have the "inside track" on information which nobody else possesses. If practically nobody jumped off a cliff, would you?
4. Professor Harold Hill is a good crowd stirrer. He uses the kind of language which sways large groups of people – mobs. He uses many different propaganda techniques. We could call his general method of manipulating *mob appeal*.
5. Answers will vary.

 Colophon

The illustrations of "Toodles" the detective,
and the art for *Nuna and Toodles*,
are by Johannah Bluedorn.

The book was designed by Nathaniel Bluedorn.
design.bloomingthorn.com

Our copyeditor was Mary Jo Tate.

The font used is Adobe Caslon Pro.